B   Charles, H.
CHARLES   Robert.

Last man out

$16.95   g

DATE			

LAST MAN OUT

LAST MAN OUT

H. Robert Charles

EAKIN PRESS
Austin, Texas

Published in the United States of America
By Eakin Press, P.O. Box 23069, Austin, Texas 78735

ISBN 0-89015-647-6

Library of Congress Cataloging-in-Publication Data

Charles, H. Robert.
    Last man out / by H. Robert Charles.
        p.   cm.
    Bibliography: p.
    Includes index.
    ISBN 0-89015-647-6 : $16.95
    1. Charles, H. Robert. 2. World War, 1939–1945 — Concentration camps — Burma. 3. World War, 1939–1945 — Prisoners and prisons, Japanese. 4. World War, 1939–1945 — Personal narratives, American. 5. Prisoners of war — Burma — Biography. 6. Prisoners of war — United States — Biography. I. Title.
D805.B9C47   1988   88-30973
940.54'72'520959 — dc19   CIP

The following is dedicated to Dr. Henri Hekking, Den Hague, Netherlands, who loved and respected his Texan friends, risking his life repeatedly to save them, although he had never seen the United States of America.

It is dedicated to those whom the Japanese held captive in Burma during World War II, forcing thousands to face acts of ultimate human indignity — death by starvation, sicknesses, firing squads, beheadings, bayonetting, beatings, and torture. It is unconscionable to allow future generations to forget what happened on the Burma railroad, just as it is to turn our backs on the holocaust in Europe.

If there is any reason to recall what happened in Hiroshima and Nagasaki each August 6 and 9, then at the same time let us remember Burma and the Death Railroad, where an estimated 100,000 prisoners died in fourteen months at the hands of the Japanese.

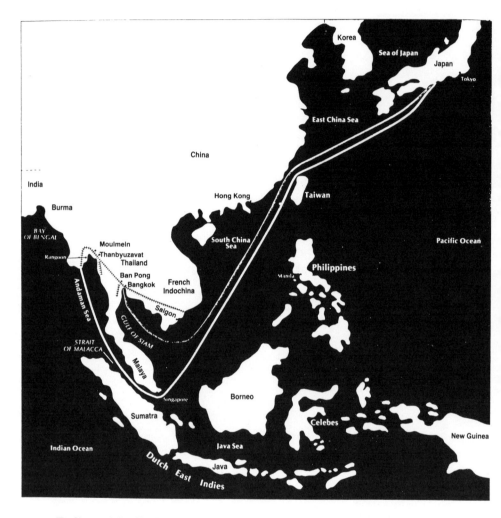

Railroad built for the Japanese by American, British, and Australian prisoners of war.

Contents

Preface

Henri Hekking saw himself as a doctor, doing what doctors were supposed to do: save lives. There was nothing heroic about it, he felt — even though hundreds of Indonesians might call him "Bapak," or father, because he had risked his life for them before the war; even though hundreds of Americans in slave labor camps in Burma might single him out as the greatest hero of the war.

There was something miraculous about his knowledge of the jungle and the treatments he used; a mystery surrounding the reason he was there in the first place. Why had he allowed himself to be tortured, risking his own life repeatedly to save the lives of his fellow prisoners?

I tried to walk back along the paths he walked, asking questions I dared to ask, leaving alone the areas where further probing might have provoked nothing but more pain. I knew something about his suffering. I had been with him during the long ordeal in Burma.

Some of Dr. Hekking's treatments were as old as time itself, yet so far advanced that medical researchers are just now beginning to prove the efficacy of what he knew and practiced even before World War II.

Since most of the story took place more than forty years ago, it would be impossible to remember the exact conversations, even for someone who was there to hear them. Thus much of the dialogue had to be reconstructed. I have changed some of the names, for personal reasons. And to eliminate confusion, in a few instances I have jiggled around the actual sequence of events. I make no apologies.

The story itself is true.

The heavy cruiser, U.S.S. Houston, flagship of the Asiatic Fleet, became a part of ABDA strike force early in 1942 and saw combat in battles of Makassar Strait, Java Sea, and Sunda Strait. It was sunk between Java and Sumatra by Japanese March 1, 1942, in the battle of Sunda Strait. Of 1,060 officers and men, 700 perished. The remainder were taken as prisoners and were held forty-three months by the Japanese.

— Photo courtesy Otto Schwarz

Acknowledgments

I am indebted to Loukie and Olaf Belinfante, Dr. Henri Hekking's daughter and son-in-law; to his wife, May, and to his son, Fred, for the countless hours they spent going over the manuscript. I wish to thank James W. Gee, Marvin Robinson, and Houston "Slug" Wright, my special prisoner-of-war friends who read the manuscript and compared it with their own recollections. I also want to acknowledge with appreciation Otto C. Schwarz, James Lattimore, Howard Brooks, John "Slapsy" Wisecup, Charles L. Pryor, Jr., Bert "Bird Dog" Page, Tom McFarland, Avon L. "Blue" Scarbrough, Franklin B. Torp, Walter K. Guzzy, J. B. Cole III, Horace Kirschner (deceased), Fred Quick (deceased), Crayton R. "Quaty" Gordon, Sr., Jesse F. Bumpass, and Cosby R. Sherrill for the valuable information they provided. I appreciate the time spent by Dr. Robert Fraser of Coldwater, Michigan, double-checking the medical aspects, and I am thankful to Michael Van de Walker, Coldwater, Michigan, for his guidance and support.

I am grateful to my wife, Marti, for her encouragement, and to my son, Robert Dana, for his valuable suggestions and advice.

Above all I am thankful for Dr. Henri Hekking.

Cpl. Howard Robert Charles, USMC
. . . photo of the author, taken December 1945

Prologue: August 1978

I.   The Nightmare

The American bomber is on the way. We're riding in the red caboose again, behind a string of boxcars and passenger cars, moving so fast we can't get off. Bird Dog, Caribou, Smokey, and the others sit there with frightened looks on their faces. We're dressed in dirt-colored Japanese uniforms. We dare not remove them.

The wooden seats are a dull red, the paint faded and almost gone. They are fastened to metal frames bolted to the wooden floor, where sand is rising, shifting, dancing to the bump and click of rails on the crooked roadbed. The tunnel behind gets smaller as the train races toward the safety of the one up ahead. I know we will never make it.

It's noon. It's time. I stand in the doorway, my heart pounding in my throat.

And there it comes, the four-engine plane as big as a silver-colored house, crossing the rails a half mile back, right wing down to the trees, banking, steadying itself, opening its bombay doors, heading straight toward us.

I am down on the floor, holding on to the metal frames to which the seats are fastened, shouting for the others to do the same. The door is flapping back and forth, opening and closing like the shutter of a film projector, revealing the plane in slow motion, the bombs in the bomber's belly breaking away, falling end over end. The shouting is drowned in the roar of engines, screams silenced in the awful explosion, swallowed up in the white-hot ball of fire. The train is lurching, careening wildly, trying to come to a stop.

We're off running across the gravel, across the field of rocks that look like human heads, bloodshot eyes staring without expression toward the plane. We're diving behind the faces in white marble, and the bomber is coming, fire spurting from its nose and sides, bullets stitching a path in the ground, ripping up sod and soil. It is over and gone, banking slowly and coming back, and we are the targets. The Japanese from the passenger cars are dead, dismembered, there by the tracks — blood-red cuts of meat.

Someone is waving the army blanket with "USA" in the middle. But the plane still comes, its engines the synchronized sound of death, and I'm screaming "Turn, you crazy bastard! Stop — for God's sake — stop!"

Sitting on the side of my bed, I am wet with sweat, wondering where I am, knowing in the same instant I am safe. I grope on the nightstand for cigarettes, finally lighting one, trying to stop it from shaking. The same dream exactly.

But then it dawns on me. This is 1978, twenty-nine years since the last dream.

I swear I won't let it worry me. If one worries, pretty soon one worries because he's worried, right? If one worries because he worries, then the next thing you know he's worried because he's worried because — well, it gets out of hand. Like an echo that goes on forever.

A week goes by. Every night, the same vivid detail. I am afraid to go back to sleep for fear I'll have it twice in one night. So I stay awake, pacing the floor. I'm worried despite myself. I know I can't go on this way indefinitely. I am already too tired and jumpy to be effective on the job. I'm taking these Valium pills, but I'm cutting back. I've got to cut back. I need help.

I have a special rate on this motel room near the office where I work northwest of Chicago's O'Hare Field. Back in the 1950s I was in charge of an ad agency's public relations department on North Michigan Avenue, north of the Loop, handling seventeen national accounts in the building industry. Now, twenty-five years later, two friends coax me back with a challenge and money to help them organize a new trade association in the building field. Not a long-term deal, unless I want it to be. A three-hour drive from my home in Coldwater, Michigan. I can commute back and forth on weekends to be with my wife, to help with the small company we own jointly. It will be a welcome and needed change — enjoyable, hopefully, working with friends of the national news media again.

The job is not easy when you've been away for fifteen years doing something else, like building your own company. But I can handle this, I convince myself and the men who hire me. Sure I can. The old Marine Corps spirit. Gung-ho.

I am bone tired, and as nervous as a guy in church who has just committed adultery with the minister's wife. I've got to get help. I'll talk to someone. But shrinks are expensive, even if I trusted them, which I don't.

I think of my friend, James W. "Caribou" Gee in Dallas. He was a marine, with me through part of it. He sees some of the other survivors regularly. Maybe they have some of the answers. He's vice-president of a large packaging company, always extremely busy. I've put off calling him, hoping the nightmare will go away.

I have keys to the office where I work, and I am there before 8:00, calling before my co-workers arrive. I reach Jim "Caribou" Gee at his home in Dallas. I explain briefly what's happening to me.

"Listen, Charlie, don't feel you're all alone," he says. "None of us came home unscathed. There's a guy down here you should talk to."

"A shrink?"

"No, although he might guide you to one at Veterans Administration after he talks to you. This man is trying to help. He's a Vietnam vet, with Disabled American Veterans. Has all kinds of information about our guys — you included. He's in Waco, not far from Dallas. His name is Ken Smith. He's probably wondering why you haven't already called."

"How can DAV have information about us?" I ask. "No one kept records. Not where we were."

"That's where you're wrong. This man has already interviewed many of our guys — me included. A surprising number did keep records, like dates, names of camps, names of guards. One guy got out with a complete diary. This Ken Smith is something else. Says he will never stop until he feels he has done all he can for all of us."

I let the phone go silent. Funny how things look different in broad daylight. Suddenly, I feel like a wimp with a weak streak a yard wide, allowing something like this to overtake me. I have lived with it all these years, kept it behind me successfully. So why give in to it now?

Jim picks up on the hesitation. "No excuses, Charlie. Get your ass down here. You hear me?"

"I don't know that I can take the time off."

"You can't afford *not* to take the time off."

"That guy in Waco. He wants me to talk about . . . what happened?"

"Maybe. I would think so."

"I've never talked to anyone about it, Jim."

"Not even to Marti?"

"Oh, sure, I've talked to her. She's my own wife, for Christ's sake. But not about all of it . . ."

"I'm no doctor, but Charlie, dammit, listen. You own your own company in Michigan, yet you're holding down a job in Chicago. What in hell are you trying to prove? My bet is, you're up to your ass in alligators. And you know something? You could lose it all if you mess around. And what the hell for? You don't need that second job!"

I don't answer right away.

"Sorry," he says. "It's none of my damned business —"

"We're trying to sell that business in Michigan, Jim," I tell him.

Before we hang up, Jim gives me Ken Smith's phone number at DAV. Three days later I am in Waco.

Ken Smith is a tough-looking guy: Texan, maybe fifty, rawboned, no-nonsense. We shake hands and he reels off some basic facts, letting me know he has done his homework.

"Jesus," I tell him, "I'm impressed. You know the story."

He grins. "Not all. I haven't heard how they got you out." He motions toward a chair.

"British paratroops. OSS. Air Transport Command," I tell him. I sit down and lean forward.

I am aware that he is watching my hands, every move I make. I am trembling, trying like hell not to show it.

"I'm glad you're here," he says, finally. "Jimmy Gee, Marvin Robinson, Charley Pryor — others talk about you. I know it's difficult, just deciding to come here. Don't worry, I'm not going to grill you about your experiences. But it will help if I know what's going on right now, okay? What size is the office you are working in?"

"Dimension? Number of people? What do you mean?"

"Dimension. How big?"

"Small," I tell him. "Maybe half as large as this. I moved into it three weeks ago. It's a postage stamp, but it's only temporary, while my regular office is being redecorated. Why?"

"Does it have a door on it?"

"Of course. What are you driving at?"

"Do you close it?"

"Not unless I have to — which is much too often."

"It bothers you to have it closed?"

I am perspiring just thinking about it. "Hell, yes!"

"How do you feel about elevators?"

"The same way. But each time I go inside one I tell myself it's not for very long, so —"

"Is there an elevator where you work?"

"No." I think this needs explaining. "There were elevators at 52 Vanderbilt Avenue in New York City where I worked as an editor before we moved to Michigan. The ones there didn't bother me as long as we had the elevator operators. Those operators were always friendly. Our offices were on the second, third, fourth, and fifth floors. Mine was on the fifth. They talked a lot as we rode up and down. The rides were short, and I was not bothered by the elevators until they automated them. But, hell — it was not that important."

He makes an appointment for me to see a Dr. Helen Kranston at Dallas VA Hospital the following afternoon.

II.   The Interview

Dr. Kranston's office is also small, and the first thing she does is close the door. I start sweating immediately. I want to get the hell out, but I've come a long distance, and as politely as I can, I ask her if it's okay to leave it open.

She does not look surprised. "It bothers you to have it shut?"

"Sorry."

"Okay," she smiles. "No problem." She props it open and sits back down at her desk, off to my right. Probably so she won't have to look directly into my face. A tall, striking brunette, probably forty, she is not unpleasant to look at.

I anticipate the perfunctory questions. "I was a marine on the USS *Houston*," I tell her. "Corporal. Serial number 284977 —"

She holds up a folder. "I have that information. Let's talk about the nightmares. Is that okay?"

"Singular, not plural. One dream. The same one, over and over again."

"Do you want to tell me about it?"

I describe it in detail.

She wants to know how long I had it after World War II, and how long I had had it this time around. "What do you think may have caused it to start again?"

"I wouldn't be here if I knew the answer to that," I tell her.

We walk around the possible causes for some time, finally getting to my overworked, overfatigued state and the effects of withdrawal from Valium that I might be having.

She asks more questions: Am I married? Yes, to Mary Margaret Butler. How long? Since 1947. Children? Yes. Three. One boy, Robert Dana, an entertainer who lives in Burbank, California, married to a former beauty queen who sang with the Fred Waring Pennsylvanians. Two daughters, Marsha Anne in Amarillo and Susan Melanie in Dallas, both married to Texans. Two grandchildren — half-Texan, I add, as a weak stab at levity.

"Do you feel you have a happy marriage?"

"Yes. Very much so."

"You feel your wife is supportive?"

"My, yes!"

"You feel you've been successful in business?"

"Up to a point . . ."

"Tell me a little about that."

I tell her all I think she needs to know. "I never really felt I succeeded," I say.

"By whose standard?"

"Mine. I had potential. I never fully used it."

"How many people do?"

"I don't know the answer to that."

"You weren't fired in New York?"

"No. I never missed a day of work because of alcohol. I did my job. They never suspected."

"You feel you had a problem with alcohol?"

"My wife finally threatened to leave me if I didn't stop drinking. To me, that was one helluva problem."

"That's why you stopped?"

"No. You don't stop drinking because of threats, or fear. I was sick of being sick, tired of being tired. Disgusted with myself. That's why I quit."

We sit in silence for a few minutes. I am too embarrassed to look at her.

"Did you ever ask yourself why you drank to excess in the first place?"

"I know when I first started it was to blot out the war. But that became just another crutch, another reason to continue drinking."

"You had this same nightmare for several years following the war. Were you in the hospital?" she asked.

"Part of the time. In Great Lakes Navy Hospital."

"How long?"

"A month, approximately."

"How did you feel? What was wrong?"

"I couldn't stand it when it got too quiet. I couldn't bear to have anyone touch me. I couldn't stand sudden noises. If I saw two or more people walking down the street make a quick move together in one direction, my impulse was to dive for cover. My heart would start pounding and I was afraid it was out of control, and then I was afraid because I was afraid because I was afraid — ad nauseum. It was like a room where mirrors are placed to make your image repeat and repeat forever."

"At the hospital, did they tell you the diagnosis?"

"Not exactly. It was written on a form attached to the foot of my bed, so I saw it. Combat fatigue, it said, at first. Then reactive depression."

"Did you know what 'reactive depression' meant?"

"I walked over to the hospital library and looked it up. Then I knew."

"You were having the nightmare then?"

"Yes."

"And you talked to the navy psychiatrist about it?"

"No. I told him nothing."

Her eyes dart toward me. "Nothing?"

"Not about the dream. I just told him I was nervous and depressed."

"Why didn't you tell him about the dream?"

"It wasn't considered smart. I wanted out of the Marine Corps. I wanted no medical history, particularly psychological."

She sat looking at me. I couldn't tell what she was thinking. I went on. "I was told that a medical history would prevent me from getting a job. It was as simple as that," I said.

"Who told you that?"

"Other patients. It was common knowledge."

"So that's why there's very little on your record. How were you discharged?"

"The circumstance?"

"You must have requested a discharge from someone."

"Yes. From the navy captain, the psychiatrist. He came around the ward one day, asking if anyone played chess. I told him I did, and he asked if I would teach him, and I volunteered. I knew it was some kind of test, and since I wanted out of the Corps I saw this as a possible way to help facilitate it. Since I was on open-gate liberty and could come and go as I pleased, I had taken the entrance exams at Northwestern University. They had notified me that I was accepted, and I wanted out of the Marines in time to start the winter quarter."

She smiles. "So, did you teach the captain how to play chess?"

"It was a farce, of course. But I started. After the third so-called lesson he told me he didn't think there was much wrong with me. Of course, I let him know I knew he already knew how to play the game. He wanted to know what kind of discharge I wanted. I told him I had passed the entrance exams at Northwestern and I wanted a straight honorable discharge, nothing on it about a medical or psychological problem, and I wanted out right away."

"You said that moments of quiet bothered you, as did certain noises. Did they ever give you any treatment for nerves?"

"No. They did try a rehab experiment once. There was this little sailor they had promised to send home for Christmas then changed their minds about him, deciding he was not ready. He was hopping mad, of course. Distraught would be a better word. They took the two of us to this fancy home on the North Shore of Chicago, into this huge living room with a roaring fireplace. We were to play bridge with these two attractive college girls. It was a terrible idea."

"Why was that?"

"Whoever set the thing up knew nothing about our backgrounds. I came from a wheat farm in Kansas. This kid came from a dirt farm in Missouri. We had never been inside a house as fancy as that. War or no war, we would have been like fish out of water. And those two girls. I hadn't been around any females for more than forty-four months. All they did was talk-talk-talk that small talk, about their hair, their latest shopping sprees and their cars, and all we could do was sit there and stare at their tender skin, their mouths and beautiful teeth and eyes, marvel at the way they were put together, and wish like hell we could get them to bed. They had me sitting in the corner, and after a while the heat from the fireplace, the perfume, the tension from trying to act normal while all the time I was feeling like a stranger peeking in on life, it got to me. I stood up with the card table and cups and saucers and whatever else was on it and I yelled and threw the whole damned mess into the middle of the living room floor, and I tried to walk out."

I realize now I am sweating profusely. Dr. Kranston hands me a tissue. "What did you yell?"

"I don't remember."

"Do you remember what happened next?"

"The two corpsmen grabbed me and strongarmed me and took me back to the hospital. I resisted, and they tried to put me in a straight jacket."

"Did they succeed?"

"No. That little sailor — he may have weighed a hundred pounds soaking wet — he says to those corpsmen, 'You'll put this guy in a straight jacket over my dead body!' And the fight was on. We were kicking hell out of those two corpsmen before this navy nurse shows up. Nurse Barbara Fisher. Full lieutenant. Tougher'n hell. But fair. And compassionate."

"Was there ever an incident with a real caboose?"

The question is totally unexpected.

My mouth is dry. I try to swallow. "Yes."

Again she waits. I feel she is watching me, but I don't want to look at her. At last she says, "Do you want to talk about it?"

I shake my head. "I don't think so."

"It might help if you do."

I shake my head. "Please."

She waits for a few more moments. "Did you strike up an acquaintance with the navy nurse?"

"Yes. She helped me over the rough spots during the rest of the time I was in the hospital. We dated for several weeks. We were engaged to be married."

"Between you, was there —?"

"It was not a sexual relationship."

"Is she your wife?"

"No. We both realized I had mistaken my gratitude for love. She said it often happened with patients. We broke off amicably."

"Was there some kind of train in your war experience?"

I know what she is after. "Yes," I tell her.

"Freight trains?"

A cold vice clamps tight on my gut. I don't answer.

She changes the subject. "If you could name one thing that helped you survive the ordeal, what would it be?"

"Thing? Or person?"

"Either. Both. Whichever."

"God, Dr. Henri Hekking, and a lot of luck," I tell her.

Again we sit in a kind of strained silence. It lasts for some time. She has stopped making notes, and I know she is studying my face. I look away.

"How did you feel about being a prisoner of war?"

The pain in my chest moves down across my gut. "You mean —?"

"Just tell me how you felt about it."

"Guilty," I tell her. "Like I let the Corps down."

"Do you still feel that way?"

"When I think of it, yes."

"Even though you were on a ship that was sunk and, according to this record, you swam . . ."

The old feelings are back, like how I compromised myself, and now, by sitting here, I'm a lily-livered, spineless wimp, letting my family down.

The choking sensation starts in my throat and is moving up, and my body is shaking again, and without warning I am crying. A damned baby! I am repulsed, mortified. Dr. Kranston shoves another Kleenex into my hands and she is saying something like

"Don't worry, it happens among the others, too, when they come in and sit right there where you're sitting."

What she says doesn't help a damned bit. I want to get the hell out of this office and never come back. I lash out at her. "Is this how you get your kicks? Watching grown men cry?"

She looks at me with sad eyes.

"Sorry," I manage, when at last I am under control. "I feel like a stupid ass."

She acts like she doesn't hear. "You feel your belief in God was the thing that helped the most?"

"Possibly. I never lost faith, even though sometimes I prayed to other deities just to cover my bets. But God expected a lot. I don't think I could have just prayed and believed and expected to survive. You had to do something. No one went around wearing religion on his sleeve, proclaiming to everyone he was a man of God. Someone would have done him in."

"Dr. Hekking? Do you want to talk about him?"

"He was a mystery. It would take all day to tell you about him."

"You were a writer in New York and Chicago. Have you ever thought of writing about Hekking? About the war?"

"Sure. I tried, once. I couldn't do it."

"Do you see your friends from the war often?"

"No. I avoid them. All except Jimmy Gee. When the navy doctor told me to put the war behind me, I assumed he meant the guys as well. So that's what I've tried to do."

"Rather than put it behind you, you should have done just the opposite. From here on, bring it out in the open. Talk about it as much as you can, particularly with your war buddies. Try writing about it again. Go into as much detail as you can. Concentrate on parts that hurt the most. Write about Dr. Hekking, if he had such a major role. That incident about the caboose. Try writing about that. If it bothers you, you can always stop. But not if you don't begin . . ."

After one interview, the nightmare ordeal abruptly ended. I don't know why. I wasn't about to analyze it, or tempt its return by reliving the past, or by talking to more psychiatrists — not even to Dr. Kranston.

I didn't start to write the story about Dr. Hekking until five years later. James Gee and his wife Shirley had a lot to do with it.

"If you don't tell it, it may never be told," Gee insisted. "No one will ever know what Hekking did, and the Japanese atrocities may be swept under the carpet and forgotten." He said he knew I would not do a Japanese-bashing kind of thing. None of us wanted that. His argument was that I was one of the few survivors who had professional writing experience. I owed it to "the guys."

He was not a VP of sales for nothing. I made a tentative start. I tried not to get too close, attempting to write it from Dr. Hekking's viewpoint, in third person, using a phony name instead of my own. An editor in New York saw an early draft and said it was potentially a great story, but it would never work unless I put myself entirely into it and made it my own deeply personal story. My first reaction was, bullshit, what the hell did he know? But another person I respect, Jane Cushman, a literary agent in New York City, told me, "You'll have to remove the bloody mask, you know, and write it in first person." She was right, of course. But now I was trapped: I had to relive the experience, starting at the beginning.

Part One

"The Lord said to Cain, where is Abel, your brother? And he said, I do not know. Am I my brother's keeper?"

Genesis 4:9

1

Sundown in Java Sea

We were losing the war in the South Pacific.

It was right after our Pacific fleet was crippled by the Japanese surprise attack on Pearl Harbor, Hawaii, December 7, 1941. We didn't realize it at the time, of course, but those of us who were already out there would be the first ones to pay the terrible price for our country's unwillingness to arm itself until it was almost too late. We knew very little about international politics, the world, or about our own country, for that matter. We were young, so very young.

We (the enlisted personnel) didn't know that, following the attack on Pearl, Japan in less than ninety days had already taken control of 27.5 million square miles of land and sea — everything from the Aleutians to the Solomon Islands 5,500 miles to the south; everything from a point near Midway Island to Malaya, 5,000 miles to the west.

In short, the USS *Houston*, the ship I was on, and every other Allied warship in the area were as fish already trapped in Japan's net, even before we fired the first shot.

The Dutch cut off Japan's access to oil in the Dutch East Indies, and Japan's reaction was to seize the oil reserves in Saigon,

15

French Indochina. France could do nothing to stop them. The United States might have, but didn't. A war was raging in Europe. The attention of the American people was focused on that. The United States was trying to negotiate a peaceful solution in the Far East when it should have been arming itself instead for Japan's impending aggression. Of course, hindsight is always sharper.

Unopposed, Nippon occupied Thailand and Cambodia, moves of a clever, determined chess player, positioning pieces to move south across Malaya, northward into Burma, India, and China.

Sir Winston Churchill read the signals and dispatched two of England's finest warships — the *Prince of Wales* and the *Repulse* — to bolster defense of Singapore. The heavy, long-range guns of Singapore were permanently mounted in concrete, pointing outward to repel raiders who might approach from the sea. Singapore was the Gibraltar of the Far East, caught with its pants down. Both British ships were promptly sunk by Japanese torpedo bombers, and the enemy did not approach from the sea but instead came down across Malaya, rendering the long-range guns useless.

It appeared that Japan would strike Australia before the United States could help defend it by sending the necessary aircraft, arms, and troops.

But that's where we came in: standing between Japan's strike force and Australia, like gnats on the back of an elephant.

"We" were the Americans, the Dutch, the British, and the Australians who fought on land and sea around and on the tiny islands of Java, Sumatra, Borneo, Celebes, and Timor — islands that made up the Dutch East Indies; islands that dot the Pacific like tiny stepping stones tossed out between the continents of Asia and Australia.

"We" were the Allied fleet dubbed ABDA — American, British, Dutch, and Australian — leftovers of the United States Asiatic Fleet merged with a few old Allied warships, which would sail out to meet the enemy and most of them never return.

Ninety-nine other marines and I, plus 960 sailors, were on the USS *Houston* during this battle of the Java Sea. Fifteen Allied warships were involved, including three submarines. We sailed against sixty of Japan's finest.

I saw it all from the vantage point of a machine-gun platform high on the foremast of the *Houston.*

We attacked the left wing of the Japanese fleet off the north coast of Java, in the Java Sea. I remember hearing discussions beforehand that since the islands were a Dutch colony it was only logical that a Dutch admiral be in command. I was one of Admiral Hart's marine orderlies when he was aboard the *Houston,* at that time the flagship of the Asiatic Fleet. So I was aware that the navy had sent him back to the United States, and that ABDA was now under the flag of the Dutch, flying from the Dutch ship *De Reuter.* Presumably our officers knew, but the common grunt like me didn't know how outnumbered and outgunned we were until early that afternoon, February 26. Then we saw the enemy's ships for the first time, sailing off our starboard side, tiny dots along the horizon as far as the eye could see. I felt a numbing fear creep across my gut and stay there, like a dinner that would never digest. I wasn't aware that a language headache existed until the battles were over. I learned then that our charts of the Java Sea were printed in Dutch, and that none of our men could speak or read Dutch. Nor could any of the Dutch speak English fluently enough to be understood in the heat of battle. We had had no time to rehearse together.

Commands were confused at the outset. When the Japanese lobbed a shell on the British *Exeter,* the ship alertly dropped out of formation to minimize the risk of damage to the rest of ABDA, and although Admiral Doorman of the *De Reuter* ordered the other ships to stay in formation, no one apparently understood. They veered off to follow, almost colliding, and ABDA went from offense to defense within seconds, never to regain the initiative.

The way I remember it, six ABDA destroyers went down. Three of the five cruisers — *Exeter, De Reuter,* and *Tromp* — were sunk. Admiral Doorman went down with his country's flagship.

Thousands perished that afternoon and evening, February 27, 1942, in the biggest sea battle since Jutland.

Despite all the losses, ABDA did manage to inflict damage, and from all accounts, it may have been responsible for stopping Japan's power surge to the south. We had lost the battle, yet, ironically, we may have stemmed the tide.

Japan's navy was stretched from Japan south like a long, tight rubber band, and only a modicum of opposition may have been all that was needed to cause her to rethink her options. There were squabbles between the Japanese army and navy about how far to go, the heavy side of the argument in favor of taking Burma first, then Australia.

Our heavy cruiser, the *Houston,* and the Australian light cruiser, HMAS *Perth,* managed to survive the fighting that extended into the night off Java — so close to shore that the three American submarines could not join the fight because of shallow water.

The worst was yet to come. There was no way to know what lay ahead. It was just as well.

Most of us on the *Houston* had enlisted prior to the outbreak of World War II because we needed food, shelter, and spending money. There were few jobs to be had in the late 1930s, or until the United States went to war. There were no such things as student loans from the federal government for those trying to finish college. The armed services provided one of the few options we had.

A young palm reader in Los Angeles told me I would take three voyages, and on the third one the ship I was on would sink. I laughed about it at the time. Her prediction didn't help much when I thought about her during those battles at sea.

The Japanese fully expected strong resistance on Java itself, the island they wanted most of all among those that made up the Dutch East Indies. They established footholds on Timor and Sumatra, placing Java in the jaws of a vice, and they were now about to disgorge as many as a hundred thousand soldiers ashore to quickly overrun the island. Only the USS *Houston* and the HMAS *Perth* remained to threaten the success of such an objective.

I had been aboard the *Houston* since June 1941. It was February 28, 1942. I remember how it felt that afternoon when we sailed into Batavia's Tanjong Priok harbor, with one compartment flooded on the starboard side by a shell we had taken below waterline, and a similar size compartment flooded deliberately on the port side to balance the ship. We were dangerously low on fuel and ammunition. Above all, we were tired. We had been on our guns more than sixty hours without sleep or rest; we had gone for many weeks with no more than catnaps stolen between Japanese air attacks. We needed rest and an ordinary, uninterrupted meal as much as anything else. We had already lost Number Three turret

— one-third of our long-range firepower — in an air attack February 4 in Makassar Strait. The raid had cost the lives of sixty crewmen, and had brought injuries to twice that many.

But there was no rest in Tanjong Priok. Still smoldering from Japanese bombs, the docks were deserted. There was no sign of humanity. A lone, hungry-looking dog nosed expectantly in a pile of rubble. The smell of burned rubber hung in the air, a grim omen of disaster.

There was much I didn't know then about the Dutch Colonial Army and why the Dutch were not available at the dock that afternoon. Having gone through the ordeal as a naive enlisted man, I know now that I should have learned as much as possible about the geo-political history of every island, every country I visited. It would have prevented bitterness later on had I known that the Dutch Colonial Army was not made up entirely of Dutch. Practically all enlisted men were natives of the islands — Indonesians who were not that loyal to the Dutch. When the Japanese invasion became imminent, the natives quickly threw away their weapons and uniforms and took off to the jungles. The Dutch, too, were gone from the docks that day, but for different reasons: some to help man the antiaircraft guns and shore batteries; others, to fight the invaders any way they could. Some were middle-aged businessmen, more business-oriented than military, but willing to lay down their lives, nevertheless, if that was what it took.

I was not aware that a Texas National Guard Battalion, 131st Field Artillery, was inland on Java, guarding an airport and a few P-40s and other assorted aircraft. Apparently, the planes had taken off and had flown away. We had wondered why there were no Allied planes in the air.

At least the fuel pumps were intact. Sailors from both ships were sent ashore to attempt the refueling normally carried out by the Dutch. This left us tied to the dock like sitting ducks, the *Houston* with a crew of 1,060 sailors and marines, the *Perth* with 682.

Most of the marines were standing by on the antiaircraft guns, squinting at the sky, sweating, expecting Japanese bombers at any second. We had no radar. All we could do was scan the sky with telescopes and binoculars, hoping we didn't see anything.

In the long rays of the afternoon sun we pulled away from the dock, the air tense enough to slice with a knife. We left Tanjong Priok with no more ammunition than we came in with, no air protection, no reconnaissance, and only vague intelligence reports. What we did have was fuel, as well as an urgent reason to reach Australia in the quickest, most direct way possible — hopefully without being spotted, without engaging the enemy.

Capt. Albert Rooks chose to go through Sunda Strait, the body of water between Java and Sumatra, then head south by southeast across the Indian Ocean to Australia.

We were following the *Perth* when the Japanese reconnaissance plane swooped down out of low-flying clouds and roared away on our port bow, lost in another cloud bank before we could bring our guns to bear. The hope that we could slip through Sunda Strait unseen was gone.

2

Sunda Strait

The *Houston* was still a formidable fighting force, despite the loss of its Number Three turret. It could bring to bear six 8-inch guns mounted in the two remaining turrets left from the air attack, these manned by navy gun crews with 4-0 ratings. It also had eight 5-inch guns manned by the marines, two 4-barrel 1.1-inch "pom-poms" manned by navy gun crews, and the eight .50-caliber machine guns — four on the forward mast, four on the after mast. The ship also had the ability to launch depth charges.

But now we were making a run for it, and the last thing we needed was another fight.

My battle station was on the machine-gun platform near the top of the forward mast. There were two men on each of the four guns, one with earphones in contact with Sky Control Forward, the pod with direction-finding equipment on the very top of the mast.

The deck of the machine-gun platform was no bigger than twenty by twenty feet. The thin shield around its perimeter was armpit high, not intended to stop shrapnel or bullets but to keep you from falling overboard. It was not a safe place to be in combat; but then, neither was any other place on the ship. I chose to be here, rather than below decks as an ammunition loader. I didn't want to guess what was going on.

Master Sergeant Standish, a World War I veteran, was in charge of the machine guns. My gun was Number Four, next to Sgt. J. M. "Egghead" Lusk on Number Two. He was the kind of tough, intelligent guy who gave the marines their reputation.

When I reached the platform the two were looking at the tiny islands in the strait, Standish wagging his head.

"What is it?" Lusk asked.

Standish scowled. "Nothing, yet. But they could hide a battle-ship out there, and we'd never see it until it attacked."

To me, the islands were a welcome sight, after fighting in the open sea.

"If we sink, at least there's land nearby," I said.

"Yeah," said Standish, "but they're not as close as they look. If you have to swim, don't try for one of those small islands. The undertow will suck you under. Go for Java, that island there to the left. It's a good ten miles away, but it's a safer bet."

"It doesn't look that far," I said.

"Take my word for it," Standish said. "Distance is always deceiving when you look out across water."

The Japanese had doggedly tracked us ever since the attack on Pearl. By their own accounts they had sunk us twice already. We had lost count of the number of times they had tried to destroy us with squadrons of bombers using pattern bombing techniques. They had intensified their efforts lately, with their large fleet moving ever closer to the East Indies. It was a miracle we were still afloat.

As darkness fell, Java seemed even farther away. I fixed it below a star formation I could easily identify, and I told myself I would do this each time I awakened during the night. We were trained to always know where our exits were.

Lusk and I had finished eating in an almost empty galley, carrying food in our hands on our way back to the forward mast, walking along the starboard railing of the main deck. The tiny islands were bathed in starlight now, and beneath scattered clouds they looked like long, gray ships lying at anchor.

Lusk asked an ensign standing by the rail if he thought we could make it through without engaging the enemy.

"It's possible, but we can't be sure. That Jap recon — God, we should have got him! There's a carrier at the other end of this. Maybe two. They know we're on the way. They'll hit us with everything they've got, dive bombers no doubt, at first light."

It was not a comforting thought. There were no comforting thoughts out there.

Pfc Miller and I were to take over Number Four at midnight. We believed there might be time for two or three hours of sleep. We decided it would be easier to rest beside the gun rather than have to run all the way up from the marine compartment the instant something started.

The padding of the kapok lifejackets protected our sides from the steel platform, which was corrugated to keep a person from sliding around. We pulled the holsters and .45s around over our stomachs so they wouldn't poke us in the ribs. We used our steel helmets for pillows, and we stretched out on our backs near the base of the gun mount. I checked the time. It was 2100 hours (9:00 P.M.). A cool breeze touched my face. As tired as I was, I couldn't sleep.

I reviewed in my mind the reasons I was in such a situation — how it was that I joined the marines in the first place.

I remembered that Friday morning, September 1, 1939, when German troops invaded Poland. I lived with the Buckleys then, two miles north of the little village of Partridge, Kansas, population 192, in almost the geographical center of the United States. We heard the news by radio. To me, it meant very little.

No one in town except J. B. Garrison, principal of Partridge Rural High, was worldly enough to know the significance. He knew that England and France had signed the "Stop Hitler" pact, and that Hitler's move meant war. There were other smart people around, like Reverend Richards of Community Church; Miss Brickey and Miss Garner, who taught English; Lyle Anderson and Dick Evans of the school board. But as far as the teenagers were concerned, it would have meant very little if all of Europe were aflame.

We lived in our own cocoons, taking our freedoms for granted. We smelled of Burma-Shave and Lifebouy, of overalls and sweat, and we went to school with our guts full. Europe, Asia, Africa, and the islands of the South Pacific existed only on maps and in the fertile minds of Hollywood scriptwriters. Few farm kids messed around very much with geography books.

Even Hutchinson, Kansas, fourteen miles to the northeast,

was a distant city. You visited for groceries and farm supplies once a week on average, usually on Saturdays. It was a rare treat when you drove that far to see a movie; a once in a lifetime event when you drove in to a dance. Only teenagers of the very rich had their own automobiles to drive when and where they chose, and no such teenager lived around Partridge. The family auto was a privilege, not a right, and you borrowed it only for special occasions — that is, if you had a family.

Rural electrification came to that part of Kansas in 1934. Television was still on the drawing boards. There were chores to do, morning and night, for kids my age. As long as I lived at the Jim Evans place, there were twenty-three cows to milk two times a day, 365 days a year, and hogs to slop, wood to split and carry in for the cookstove, milk to be separated into cream and butter. These jobs were never finished before 9:00 each night. It was impossible to read very much after that without falling asleep.

I ran away from the Evans place when I was sixteen. I had no real family after that, although the three Buckley ladies for three years were the nearest thing to it.

Ruby and Myrtle taught grade school and lived with their mother, Maude. I lived with the three of them on their small farm until just after I graduated from high school. They said they needed help with chores around the farm. As it turned out, they had no livestock, only a few chickens, and what crops they had were planted, tilled, and harvested by their brothers who farmed nearby. Actually, there were few chores to do except in summer when I helped the younger brother, Ted, with wheat harvest. Even then, he insisted on paying me so I'd have some extra money of my own when school resumed.

What the Buckleys did have in abundance was love and compassion, for each other, and for me, and they expected nothing in return. They didn't make any real fuss over me, and I was grateful for that.

Their farm was a safe haven from a stepfather who delighted in beating animals and humans alike. The Buckleys apparently understood me, so there was no need to talk about it. Although I suffered the mood swings of a person rejected by his own family, if indeed I had ever had one, I had the good fortune to live in an environment of true unselfishness and kindness.

We drove into Partridge to church Sunday morning after Poland was invaded. Ruby sat up front with Myrtle, who was driving the 1936 Terraplane; Mrs. Buckley and I were in back. Mrs. Buckley said, "That Adolph Hitler. I declare. I just knew he was up to no good."

Myrtle was listening to the car radio. "Don't you worry about him, Mother. England, France, Canada, Australia, and New Zealand — even the Union of South Africa — have just declared war on Germany! That will cook old Hitler's goose!"

Almost everyone who attended the little community church arrived early to visit before services began. In good weather, the men lingered by the front steps, talking, while the women went inside. J. B. was holding forth by the steps that morning, talking about the war spreading across the whole of Europe, the Middle East, and Africa — most likely the United States before it was over.

"We're already sending weapons to England," J. B. reasoned. "So we'll be in it, mark my words. All the Germans have to do is sink just one of our ships carrying those weapons."

Some of the farmers shook their heads and reckoned as how he could be right. Others looked down at their shoes then looked away as though they were remembering something painful, like World War I. Harold Love, a farmer's kid my age, was there, and he and I listened, failing to see how either of us would ever be involved. But I was not to forget the look on J. B.'s face, or the uneasy feeling I had when we finally went inside.

Reverend Richards gave a prayer that morning that somehow the war "over there" would end quickly.

The Buckleys were determined that I go on to college, even though we had no money. I could at least attend Hutchinson Junior College, they insisted, believing if I studied something useful, like economics, I might have a fighting chance in the world of free enterprise. They helped me enroll and arranged for me to live at the YMCA.

The following Monday evening after school, while Hitler's army was still in the process of occupying Poland, Myrtle, Ruby, and I drove into Hutchinson to talk to a Mr. Remington who ran the "Y."

Remington helped young men like me "get back on the straight and narrow," as he called it, the presumption being that I, not my stepfather, had done something wrong. He was a huge, pink-faced man who had a patronizing way of grinning. "Your stepfather is Jim Evans?" he chortled. "The man who tried to have his neighbor arrested for stealing turkeys?"

I wondered to myself how he knew. Myrtle nudged me to speak up, to say something.

I distrusted him. I kept my mouth shut.

"It was on the front page of the Hutchinson *Herald*," Remington laughed. " 'Farmer Accuses Neighbor of Stealing Turkeys,' the headline said. All the man was doing was trying to save your stepfather's turkeys which had run away in a wind storm!"

"We didn't see the story," Ruby snapped. She was the shorter of the two sisters, and shorter-tempered. She was seething, fighting to restrain herself. "I believe we already discussed the boy's home-life in some detail," she said. "Our understanding is he will help at the desk, and you in return will provide his room and five dollars a week."

My things were in the car, and the "girls" helped me move in before Remington could change his mind. Everything I owned fit into one drawer of the small chest, except for the new green pin-stripe suit the girls had given me for my high school senior prom.

The room was barely large enough for a cot, a stiff-backed chair, and the chest of drawers topped with a washpan and a pitcher of water. The one bathroom that served the third floor was a half block down the hall. This would be my home for a year and a half.

Junior College, "Juco," was approximately ten blocks away, and in between on Fifth Street was a boardinghouse in a private home where, for three dollars and fifty cents a week, one could fill up each day at noon on meat loaf, bread, potatoes, and gravy — sometimes beef, pork, or chicken — then fight all afternoon to stay awake. My mother had sent enough money to cover the cost of text-books. The only other book I had to buy was a *Webster's Dictionary*, circa 1936 (which I still have). I could find whatever else I needed at the library. This left a dollar and a half to spend each week on beer and movies, or, if I saved for two weeks, perhaps even a date.

I made few friends at Juco. Not because of a lack of money but because there was too little time. I worked as much as five hours an evening renting rooms, selling candy, issuing towels and keys to lockers for those who came to use the athletic facilities and the showers. I spent the rest of the time studying.

On one occasion I failed to balance the books, coming up short two cents before the next person came on duty. Search as I might through cash receipts, I couldn't find where I had erred. So to avoid a reprimand from Remington, I took two pennies from my own pocket and put them into the cash drawer. But somehow Remington found out. He was like an enraged bull, mainly because I had tried to cover up my mistake.

"That's totally dishonest!" he bellowed.

"Not as bad as if I had kept the two cents," I said, lamely.

He threatened to fire me if it ever happened again. It didn't. I learned to make and record each transaction right to the penny, determined that if I ever did make another mistake I would openly admit it, no matter what the consequences. It was probably one of the best lessons I ever learned, but I suspect it was one of the experiences that destroyed forever any interest I might have had in accounting.

Three others who lived at the "Y" walked with me to the boardinghouse or met me every day at lunch: Don Lundstrum, a short, powerfully built guy who loved to play ping-pong; Lundstrum's friend, a tall skinny guy named Dave, who swore he read two or three average-length books a day; and Kenneth Ehling, who wanted to become a lawyer, and somehow you knew he would be. The three of us talked about the war in Europe.

On May 10, 1940, when German aircraft bombed the major air bases of The Netherlands without declaring war, I remember Don and Ken saying it was time to think about which branch of service we would choose before Uncle Sam did the choosing for us. Fifth Columnists were dashing for Holland's bridges, trying to prevent the Dutch from destroying them. Motorcycle troops were roaring ahead of the awesome German tanks and troops, racing to keep the Dutch from opening the dikes. We were glued to the radio, rooting for the Dutch. But it was all over in Holland in five days. Hitler's troops did what the Spanish failed to do: for the first time in 888 years the flag of a foreign power flew above Netherlands soil.

A guy named Virgil who worked with me said he was going to join the Canadian Air Force.

"I think I'm going into the marines," I announced.

That went over with a dull thud.

"You're outta your mind," said Dave. "They're the guys who get it first!"

Ken and Don joined the army. I never heard what happened to Dave.

I borrowed Ken's Model A Ford shortly after that and drove over to Partridge. Going back was becoming a kind of ritual, a pilgrimage preceding the big decisions in my life. Sometimes I'd arrive and not say why I was there. Other times, like today, I'd find J. B. and talk it out.

It was raining at noon, and there weren't many places J. B. could be. Main Street was four blocks long, and a quagmire of red glue. A filling station and two large wheat elevators stood like bookends on opposite ends of town, holding between them the rundown houses and empty lots overgrown with weeds. The post office was inside a drug store filled with the aroma of crackers, candy, and tobacco. Men sat on benches around a pot-bellied stove, whittling, spitting into the huge spitoon made probably of solid brass, although no one had ever cleaned off the hardened tobacco juice to find out. In the same building you could buy a malted milk or a milk shake at the counter next to the post office window and mail counter. J. B. sometimes went there for lunch, but he was nowhere around. He wasn't across the street at the grocery store, either. I went on over to the high school.

There were eighty students where J. B. reigned as principal and teacher of math and manual training. Partridge High was a split-level brick building, with gymnasium and music room in a half-basement, and study hall-library combination plus classrooms on the first and only other floor. There was a tennis court out back, where Bob Anderson played and beat the socks off all contenders in Class D, and an oval track beyond, where I did the half-mile in two minutes, two and two-tenth seconds, and where Don Epperson did the mile in something close to five minutes. That year, Bob, Kenneth Kraus, Don Epperson, and I won the state championship for Class D in the half-mile medley at the Kansas Relays, Kansas University, Lawrence. We ran on the same track the same day Glen Cunningham, Jesse Owens, and the Texas Rideout brothers ran in exhibitions. The four of us plus four others — Fat Love, Tom Haney, Jack Rexroad, Tom Terrell — also played on the basketball team together.

I had the great good fortune of talking to Glen Cunningham before we ran the medley at KU that day. He sat on the grass doing stretch exercises, talking to us as though we were the special ones. We were shocked to see the extensive burn scars on his legs. He asked how much I jogged to warm up before I ran the half-mile. "A couple of hundred yards, I reckon," I said. "Try a mile, at least," he said. "Run the same distance each time, before you run the 880."

After we won the race that day, and I was bent over gasping for air, I saw the outstretched hand. I reached out to take it and looked into Cunningham's smiling face. "Well done," he said.

I was never so proud in my life.

I was standing in the downstairs hall, staring into the trophy case, remembering, when J. B. came to stand beside me.

"Still looks pretty good, doesn't it?" he said, nodding toward the largest trophy, placed in the center of the case. It was the only one with my name on it, and my name was misspelled. I had never said anything. I had had my day of glory. I knew who the anchor man was that day, and I knew who was there to say "well done." That was all that mattered.

J. B. had four sons younger than I, and a daughter about my age. I wondered if he still thought the United States would go to war, and if he thought his sons would be involved. "Yes, I'm afraid so," he said.

"I think I'll join the marines," I announced, watching his face. He frowned. "Why the rush?"

"There's talk of conscription."

"They won't draft you if you go to college two more years and get your degree. Go to Kansas State, up in Manhattan. Take ROTC. Enter service as an officer."

"I have no money," I said.

"Old Jim won't help? How about your mother?"

"She'd help if she could, but . . ." I shrugged.

J. B. scowled. "Why the marines?"

I told him I had gone to the library and had done some reading about the various branches of service. If I had to go I wanted to be with the outfit that usually got there first.

J. B. knew me as well as I knew myself— probably better. He had trailed me halfway across the country to find me and bring me back to a safe haven with the Buckleys so I could finish high school.

He knew I was determined to fly away again. Only this time he wouldn't try to dissuade me.

It was to be my last night at the YMCA. The next day, Monday, June 1, 1940, I was to be on a bus to Kansas City to find the marine recruiting office.

After dinner, I went to a movie at the Fox Theater, just off Main Street, adjacent to Wiley's Department Store. I was two blocks away from the theater, walking alone on a dimly lit street near the "Y," when Jim Evans came out of nowhere, grabbed me, and pulled me between two parked cars. He was a huge man, like Remington, only much stronger. "You sonuvabitch," he muttered. "You thought you'd get away with it, didn't you?"

"What are you talking about?" I could feel myself growing numb.

"Taking that whip. Hitting me in the head! I'm gonna stomp you for that, boy. I'm gonna teach you!"

"That was two years ago," I pleaded. "I grabbed the whip because you were beating me with it."

It occurred to me to run, but I decided to hold my ground. I didn't see him swing. I felt the impact. I saw the world turn white and red — then black.

The next thing I remember is being dragged from the back seat of the car, out onto an open field. I felt like a dead animal. I knew I had better act that way. I remember the cool air, the smell of fresh dirt and tobacco spit, and the sound of heavy breathing. I lay still, fearful that if I moved he would do the job he must have thought he had done already.

After I heard the car drive away, I raised up on an elbow and looked around. I hurt all over. Lights were on in a farm house not more than a hundred or so yards away. I recognized the road as the diagonal that cut southwest out of South Hutchinson toward Partridge. I started to walk toward the house, fell two or three times before I finally gave up and, on all fours, dragged myself across the field.

I never told the people at the farm house what had happened. They helped me wash myself off, and on the way back to the YMCA the old farmer who drove the car kept asking if I wanted to go to the hospital or talk to the sheriff. I told him no, I wasn't that badly hurt, it was a private matter, and I thanked him and told him to please forget about it.

The next day I was on the bus to Kansas City.

I had gone to sleep without realizing it. Suddenly, the world was a giant fireball.

3

The Inferno

A torpedo had smashed into the screws. The *Houston* was dead in the water.

Japanese warships were pulling out from behind the tiny islands, their searchlights and starshells illuminating both sides of the ship. The two turrets were firing, first in one direction and then in the other. The two batteries of five-inch guns — eight altogether — opened fire. Then the one-point-ones, the pom-poms. Word came for the machine guns to open fire on searchlights. My machine-gun loader, Pfc Miller, was tapping me on the shoulder, signaling that a belt of ammo was in place. I pulled the cocking lever back twice and aimed at a searchlight and pulled the trigger, using the stream of tracers to guide the bullets.

Ahead, after thirty minutes of fighting, the *Perth* was sinking.

Thirty minutes after that, the *Houston* had nothing to fire but star shells and machine-gun bullets. I had lost track of the number of belts I had used.

I squeezed the handlebar trigger again and again, watching the stream of molten-red tracers disappearing into the searchlight. I raised the trajectory, spraying the bullets higher and back and forth. But the white light kept coming.

The gun abruptly stopped.

"Ammo!" I screamed into the spectre of more searchlights ringing the ship, moving in closer from all directions. "More ammo!"

I yanked up the top plate of the gun and turned to yell again for Miller. Miller was gone. So were the other six men, their guns standing gray and ghostlike, pointing in different directions. Only Standish, the gunnery sergeant, was there. Near the front end, a part of the machine-gun platform was blown away, revealing through twisted steel the top of Number Two turret a few feet below and forward. Smoke boiled through a black, gaping hole in its top. An acrid smell oozed up with smoke along the forward mast, up through the access opening to the platform and around the steel box where I bent over to pull out another belt of ammo.

I was reloading the gun when the truth hit: the slant of the deck, the deadly silence broken by voices far below, someone shouting amidships. Groans, screams, then nothing. No sounds of the main battery, no sounds of the five-inch guns or pom-poms — no noise, the worst sound of all.

The bugle — I remembered now! Twice it had blown; twice the order had come to abandon ship, and soon it would be too late.

I held my hand up to shield my eyes.

I snapped down the plate and pulled back the cocking lever. Twice. I felt the hand gripping my shoulder. "Better go, Charlie," Standish was saying. "It's all over — finished."

I squeezed the trigger. The light disappeared. But another was coming, and another.

I let go of the handlebars and looked around into the wrinkled face etched like white marble. "What about you? You going with me?"

Standish wagged his head and grinned. "I'd never make it. Go, now. Swim away before you're pulled under."

An old man, obese, unwilling to budge from a platform halfway up the main mast — Standish had said once he couldn't swim.

I leaned against the metal shield at the back of the platform and looked below, where men were sliding an orange-colored life raft over the starboard side, a side already down in the water. Fire raged in hangars aft of the quarterdeck, flames licking along the after mast. Methodically, men were jumping off the port side, the side highest out of the water, away from the undertow.

Edging toward the opening where the ladder ran along the mast, I looked back at the older man. Commander Maher, the gunnery officer, was with Standish now, nodding his head toward the ladder. "Go on," he was saying to Standish, who was shaking his head.

"Come on, Sarge," I urged. "You and me, we'll make it."

"No, Charlie. Go on."

I pointed. "It isn't very far to that island. See? There — beneath the Southern Cross."

Again Standish shook his head. Calmly, he said, "Goodbye, Charlie."

An awful shudder went through the ship. I grabbed the rungs and started down. I would try to find my friend Howard Corsberg. Corsberg couldn't swim, either. He was on the five-inch guns behind the hangar. I'd get a life raft and get him on it, and somehow we'd make it to shore together.

Down I went past the bridge and conning tower, decks strewn with bodies and crooked steel lit up like day in the searchlights. Past a groaning man with one leg torn off, the stump forming a black-red pool. Over the lifeless shapes, an arm, a hand, my shoes slipping on slime and defecation. Through the smells of fried flesh and hair, like odors of animal hides scorched by branding irons. Past the gruesome parts, leavings in a human butcher shop.

Like a fool I found myself counting — twelve, thirteen, fourteen — live people, here, breathing only minutes ago. I kept thinking, pulling back, stomach churning, realizing I was choking on my own vomit.

I went on, feeling direction, sensing purpose, body moving as if propelled by someone else.

Life rafts were stored in the hangars aft of the quarterdeck amidships. I would have to reach them. But the hangars were ablaze, and the quarterdeck was littered with dead and with men trying to reach the lifeline to hurl themselves overboard. Muzzle bursts were blinking under searchlights, and out of the darkness came the red streaks arcing in across the starboard side, ripping into bodies caught on the lifelines.

Dropping on hands and knees, I crawled to the opposite side and crouched behind the steel bulkhead. Standing there was a tall marine, grinning, smoking a cigarette: Sergeant Lusk, leaning against the lifeline. He flicked the butt over the side and watched it go down. "You ready?" he asked.

"Go ahead," I tried to say. It came out like somebody else's voice. I watched him vault over the line and go down until he splashed in the blackness below, disappeared, emerged, and began to swim away.

I could feel the heat of the roaring inferno on my back as I tightened the straps of my lifejacket, searching the sky for the Southern Cross. I reached out and grabbed the lifeline. No matter what happened, I would swim toward those six bright stars hanging over the tiny black strip of land that had to be Java.

I jumped feet first, arms clutched around my knees. I felt the explosion of water and held my breath, feeling myself going down, down into black silence. And then I kicked, struggling to move upward, feeling as though my lungs would burst. I shot through the surface and swam to distance myself from the blazing hell.

4

"Horyo!"

When I looked back, the ship was down by the bow, sinking slowly, majestically, stern and screws in the air, flag fluttering in the glare of searchlights. My body trembled in oily water. I spotted the Southern Cross and started swimming toward the tiny finger of land beneath it where I assumed the Dutch would be fighting the Japanese. I would join them, I thought, and I would fight along beside them.

The sea was thick with bobbing heads and orange lifejackets. Taking my time, I tried to keep my eyes on the six stars. Behind me a man was yelling for help, and logic told me to swim on — it was too early to know whether I could save myself, let alone help someone else. Moments later I changed my mind. I swam back. The man had no lifejacket. He was flailing the water with his arms, apparently blinded. "Take it easy," I told him. As the man got a vice-like grip on my arm, I slapped him across the face. "Take it easy! I won't let you drown. Hold on to my lifejacket. There. That's it!"

The man held on, trying to help as we swam away. Moments later his body felt heavy, and there was no sound. He had turned loose of my lifejacket, and was face down in the water. When I turned him over I saw his chest for the first time — what was left of it.

An eerie silence enveloped us. All I could hear was my own breathing and the lapping of waves against the collar of my lifejacket.

The man wore no identification tags around his neck, no ID bracelet on either wrist. I wondered if I should search his pockets for some kind of ID then report his death. But to whom would I report it? It looked like a long way to shore.

I searched him. Apparently, he had rushed to his battle station without identification.

The Southern Cross was still there, cold and indifferent. I turned loose of the man and swam away. I didn't look back.

Hours later, daylight was coming. My wristwatch was gone. I had no way of knowing how long I had been in the water.

I felt my energy draining away as I stopped swimming to look at the long line of troopships strung out to infinity, at landing barges taking troops to the beach, returning high in the water, empty.

It was difficult now just to stay afloat. I unlaced my field boots and let them go. I took off the belt and let it go with the .45 and holster. Soon the lifejacket too would have to go. It was waterlogged all the way up to the collar.

Soldiers along the rail of a ship were yelling, taunting, trying to get me to yell back. A ladder was lowered for another swimmer who threw off his lifejacket, caught the lower rung, and started climbing. The Japanese sailors let him get halfway up before they threw him back, laughing as if it were some kind of joke.

"Can you make it?" I yelled to the man.

His head bobbed in the water, then disappeared.

The ship came closer than I had estimated it would. I altered my course to keep it from plowing into me. The sailors were taunting, encouraging me to grab the rope ladder. I swam from it with all the strength I could muster, feeling the presence of the steel hull moving by like a giant piece of land.

"Hey, America-ga? You America?" A blur was waving and yelling from the railing.

My body felt cold and naked.

"Hey, American! I go to school in UCLA. How does it feel to lose the war?"

Like hell, I thought. Hot pain seared along the backs of my

legs, no matter how slowly I moved. I had to keep going, to reach land before I passed out.

Peering through painful slits I could make out the sandy beach, the cluster of oil-drenched men standing with hands on heads surrounded by men with machine guns. Blinding sunlight sparkled on water, reflections burning my eyeballs like millions of tiny needles. Through a hazy curtain I viewed my own body as if by some miracle I lived apart from it. I felt the water lapping into my mouth and nostrils; I sensed I was no longer able to move, yet there was no feeling of fear or panic, no longer any urgency. A war was going on in my brain, one side urging me to fall asleep, the other insisting I stay awake and keep moving. No excitement; just peaceful detachment. Try moving again, keep thinking, don't let it happen, one side of my brain was saying. You're no good when the chips are down, said a voice from still another side — a voice from another time, coming from Jim Evans's thin, twisted lips dripping with tobacco juice.

Prove you can make it, I told myself.

A voice cut through the fog: "*Kodah! Anata wa, horyo!*"

I squinted into the sun as a rope whacked across my face.

"*Anata, horyo?* You surrender-kah?"

I grabbed onto the rope, looking into the faces of the Japanese soldiers — two of them, in a motor launch — and into the black hole of a machine gun.

Somehow I was able to hold on to the rope. The engine revved and the slack went out. They were pulling me closer to land.

Moments later, the boat stopped and I felt my feet touch the ground. The man waved toward the beach. "You surrender-kah! You surrender-kah!"

I stood watching as the boat churned out toward another bobbing head farther away from shore.

There was no choice.

I struggled toward the beach, toward the knot of men who were now prisoners. *Horyos.*

5

Moving On Into Darkness

Survivors of the *Houston* were kept in jails in Serang, Java, twenty men in cells designed for six. In my cell, an open two-gallon bucket placed near the door was our only toilet facility. It was taken out, dumped, and brought back once a day. Flies swarmed. The stench was overpowering. Another bucket of the same size contained our drinking water. We had one cup, which was used by everyone. We were fed one plain rice ball once a day, and we were rapidly losing weight, starving, going into stages of depression. Since there was no bedding, huge sores developed on bony hips and shoulders from lying on bare concrete. Our wounded, unattended, were left to die.

A marine, John Shuster, lay on the concrete next to me. He was a blonde guy with fair skin who grinned a lot. When someone said he would give anything for a sandwich, John and I agreed we'd settle for just an old stale crust of bread, and we laughed as though it were the greatest joke of the week. A sailor from New Jersey talked incessantly about a stuffed pork chop his father made in their family restaurant. After several days of listening to that, John told him where he could stuff his pork chops.

One sailor wore thick glasses. He had tied them on when he jumped off the ship. "What did you do, walk on water?" someone asked him. We would find a second use for those glasses.

We had been in the cell for just over a week when another sailor joined us. He had been on a raft for three days. When he finally made it ashore, he wandered around with the natives for three more days before they took his watch and billfold and turned him over to the Japanese. The Japanese questioned him, beat him, then shoved him into the cell with us.

We let him rest an hour or so. "You got any cigarettes?" I asked.

"Wog," he said.

In answer to my question, what the hell is wog, he pulled a sack of cigars out of the inside of his shirt. They were like cigars except the ends were not tapered. They were made of tree moss soaked in tobacco juice, laid out to dry, then wrapped in green tobacco leaves. "Ever hear of a wackin' white cheroot?" he asked.

"Rudyard Kipling," I said. "You got any matches?"

He didn't, and neither did anyone else.

There was a small window ten inches high in the east wall. I borrowed the eyeglasses and used them to magnify the sun's rays to light one of the "cheroots."

Shuster said he could have told Kipling what to do with his wackin' white cheroots. They were ten times as strong as American cigarettes, and exploded several times during the course of being smoked. A drag or two on one of those, on an empty stomach, had the dizzying effect of a slug of straight booze.

Once a week we were allowed outside to bathe in a courtyard. We stood under showers while a guard watched, a fiendish grin on his face. Whether the man was homosexual or merely trying to be friendly we never knew. There was no soap or towels, so all we did actually was rinse off. It was better than nothing.

Six weeks later we were taken out of the jails, placed in the backs of open trucks, and driven up one street and down the other in central Batavia.

It was a filthy, disease-infested city. I doubt if any of us were concerned about what the citizens of Batavia thought. It was a relief to be out of the jail cells, even though we were apprehensive, wondering what the Japanese would do with us next. This parading of prisoners was supposed to bolster the image of Dia Nippon's superiority ("Look, see who we've got here, your former rulers, now our slaves!"). But I doubt if it worked. As our line of trucks moved slowly along the streets, men, women, and children went about their business for the most part, trying to ignore us. At the risk of being slapped or beaten by the Jap guards on the trucks, some were lofting bananas and cigarettes into the trucks, while others looked then quickly lowered their eyes as if embarrassed. That told us all we needed to know: that human beings, regardless of who they were, were not impressed by displays such as this.

We were finally deposited inside the huge Dutch Colonial Army garrison called "Bicycle Camp" by the Dutch, somewhere within the city limits (a huge hotel built for tourists is on that site today). This was the collecting point for prisoners of war on Java. Each of the white stucco buildings with orange tile roofs had approximately 200 small two-man cubicles, partitions ripped off so guards could watch our movements without wandering around inside.

We slept on bare concrete floors without blankets that first night in Batavia. But officers and men of the 131st Field Artillery, the Texas Army National Guard unit, were in a building across the courtyard, and they soon came to our aid. Three of their officers, Capt. Arch L. Fitzsimmons, Lt. James P. Lattimore, and Lt. David Hiner were among the first to share their personal gear, such as bars of soap, razors, mess kits, shoes, and clothing.

Two of the marine officers who survived, Lt. Frank Gallagher and Lt. Edward Barrett, were taken to Japan along with the surviving navy officers. Thus we soon adopted Lattimore, Hiner, and Fitzsimmons for our own. Their personalities were as different as their appearances — Lattimore short and thin with light blue eyes and sandy hair, Fitzsimmons six-feet-two, with dark brown hair and short-cropped mustache. Those of us weaned in the Corps had little confidence in any officer who did not look the part. And neither of these men could have passed the superficialities of a marine parade ground inspection. They did not have the military bearing. So we tried to pretend they didn't exist, at first. This, too, would change.

Bicycle Camp became a Japanese boot camp for prisoners of war. They fed us rice and soup, an improvement over plain rice. But what they wanted to do was to bring us down to submission.

We were first made to bow and salute our new "masters" — all Japanese, regardless of rank. To them, bowing had been a custom for centuries, a way of expressing honor and respect. The deeper and more prolonged the bow, the greater the respect. Had we known this, no doubt we would have taken it in stride, rather than regard it as a humiliating thing to have to do. It was the method they had of enforcing such a custom that made it even more degrading. With few exceptions, no one in the military had ever been slapped in the face, beaten, or made to act like a slave for a simple infraction of discipline. But brutality now became a way of life.

If one hesitated — or even looked as though he resented having to bow or salute — punishment was swift in coming and it seemed to last forever. One did not have to disobey an order to be beaten. It could happen at any moment, and often did, for no reason at all.

The Japanese soldier placed great emphasis on his masculinity, lowering his voice several notches by force to make it sound deeper, meaner, and harsher. He strutted, pulling the corners of his mouth down like an actor in a Kabuki play. He appeared to engineer his anger, starting at one level and building his rage to the point of explosion. If you never hated before, you did now. But you could not let it show, if you wanted to live.

Some rules were vague and never fully explained. For example, we were never to be within less than five paces of the fence. What constituted five paces? Differing lengths of measuring tape existed in the minds of every guard. There was no way to anticipate when one would be singled out, or of guessing what the severity of punishment would be. And you worried about your own reaction, until you were beaten the first time. How would you act? Would you appear to be weak before your friends? Would you cry out for mercy?

Our "masters" wanted to be feared. They conducted themselves in ways to make you afraid. They expected it. They needed it. If one did not at least act like he was afraid of them, he was either stupid or doomed to be beaten to death.

I didn't know who else besides me had already experienced physical abuse.

I had better explain that, because there may be some psychological significance. My full name is Howard Robert Charles. I've never liked the name Howard because, somewhere in the back of my mind, I still dislike that period in my life when I was called Howard, when I allowed Jim Evans to beat me. I didn't respect myself at the time for taking it, and for watching him beat my young half brother, Mike, and not trying to defend him. I used to fantasize about fighting Jim — even killing him. Of course, it was only a fantasy. My method of coping was to run away.

I was lucky to have had the Buckley family. Mike stayed and took it. Jim did not allow him to finish high school, much less go on to college, whereas I managed to do both.

No doubt a few others at Bicycle Camp had experienced similar beatings, if they came from troubled homes. Ironically, I think it helped me to deal with the Japanese beatings.

While I concentrated on not hating the Japanese people as a whole for the treatment I got from a few, I despised the Japanese soldiers and the way the guards conducted themselves. Every sane, civilized person in the world felt the same revulsion I did when I learned of the way the Japanese militants used women and children for bayonet practice in China.

The bad that comes to one's life is often balanced with good. I firmly believed that. I was never abnormally afraid of the Japanese, one on one. Part of it was Marine Corps training, but I'm certain it was mainly because of the other "special" training administered by Jim Evans. I knew how to take the punchings and slappings, letting a guard get his kicks out of thinking he was hurting me. That's the way I had handled myself with my stepfather. "Howard," he would say. "I'm gonna fix you, you little sonuvabitch." And then he would beat me, always in private, sometimes with fists, sometimes with that blacksnake whip, promising to kill me if I ever so much as breathed a word about it to my mother particularly, or to anyone else. I know there was some kind of sadistic delight he got from doing it.

I reacted to the guards who beat the prisoners as I did to my stepfather. I would never deliberately antagonize them. I would let them get their kicks from beating me, and I would wait, and one day . . .

I was struck in the face with a four-cell flashlight for not saluting. It made me angry. But I kept my composure. On another occasion, for no reason that I was aware of, a guard broke three ribs in my right side with a rifle butt. I collapsed, acting more hurt than I actually was. I believe I escaped a lot of punishment by avoiding eye contact and by acting afraid — a conduct I disliked myself for. But the name of the game was survival, to hell with false pride.

Marine 1st Sgt. H. H. Dupler got the marines together one morning to tell us what he had learned about the final battle. Of the ship's crew of 1,060, only 368 had survived. Of the 100 marines, 30 had survived and were captured.

My good friend Howard Corsberg was gone. So were so many others I knew.

"Hang in there," Dupler said. "We'll make it."

Trying to boost our morale, Dupler started leading us in close-order drills, marching us back and forth across the dirt parade ground, building a cloud of dust. Had anyone else tried to instigate such a thing, we would have told him to forget it. But we were eager to please Dupler. "Gotta stay fit, men," he growled. "Any day, now, our guys'll hit that beach out there. And by gawd we better be ready." I think he really believed the Allies would strike back that soon.

The Japanese were amused by Dupler, at first, but horrified later on when the entire camp — British, the remaining Americans, the Dutch, and the Australians — started doing their own close-order drills. The guards poured out on the grounds to stop it then, beating Dupler until he couldn't stand.

In late August 1942 approximately 150 of us were taken to the Batavia docks and shoved into the bilge of an ancient freighter used previously to transport cattle. We were so crowded we barely had room to lie down on straw soaked with urine and cow dung.

Plain rice balls were handed down through a hatch then passed along to men in the furthest reaches of the bilge, several dirty hands touching each one along the way. Predictably, diarrhea and dysentery broke out. Toilets were on the stern — makeshift four-holers built of wood, extending out over the side. Long lines formed as prisoners sought to use them. Often, they couldn't wait. Seldom did defecations drop into the sea without first splattering along the hot steel side. Soon, the ship smelled like a floating thousand-hole outhouse.

Drinking water was scarce. Unless one had a full canteen when he came aboard, he was quickly dependent upon the beneficence of others. James "Packrat" McCone, a marine survivor of the *Houston,* had approximately five gallons in a metal fuel tank, which helped save the lives of some who were too sick or weak to forage for themselves.

Houston T. "Slug" Wright of the 131st Field Artillery found hot water dripping from a steam pipe on the topside. He had started filling the canteen when a guard saw him and knocked him flat of his back, not for taking the water but for being outside of the bilge. The glasses he wore were unbroken when he picked them up off the deck. He put them back on and waited around until the guard left. Then he sneaked his canteen under the pipe again. A different guard saw him and again he was hit, managing to hang on to his glasses as he staggered backwards. This didn't stop him. He waited until after dark and went back. And persistence paid.

There was much speculation about where the Japanese were taking us. Some thought Japan. But going there would have required us to sail northward, and we could tell by the sun and stars we were heading west by northwest. Someone suggested the destination was China. A coastline was visible off the starboard side. Maybe it was Malaya.

"They're staying close so they can head for shallow water, just in case," James W. Gee said.

Gee was one of the first men I had met on the *Houston* when I reported for duty in Manila Bay, Philippines, June 6, 1941. He was a boxer, and since I wanted the routine of exercise I had asked him to teach me some of the finer points. Learning was a frustrating experience. Try as I might, I could never land a glove on him. Many called him "Caribou" because of his size: six-foot-two and 200 pounds. He was a rugged type the Marine Corps liked, an all-around athlete, a natural leader with two years of credits at The University of Texas. They had used photos of him for recruiting posters. Despite his size, education, and athletic prowess, he was a gentle person, and ironically, because of that, a marine lieutenant had passed him over for promotion.

We tried to sleep in the bilge without success. It was stifling hot and nauseating. Someone was trying to open a porthole.

"If we ever get out of this, will you stay in the Corps?" he asked.

"Me? You've got to be kidding."

"What will you do?"

"Anything else. Go back to college, if I can raise the money. Try to learn something constructive. I just want to make it, you know what I mean?"

I helped a soldier open a porthole. I stood there inhaling the salt air, looking out at the sea, thinking of my friend, Howard Corsberg. Finally, someone told me to move away. I was blocking his air supply.

When I got back to my place I asked Gee if he remembered how Corsberg liked the sea.

"Sure, I remember. He said 'up ahead is adventure, below is mystery, behind are all the memories.' "

"He was a sentimentalist, a romantic. Always commenting on the passing scene. I miss him," I said.

"Yes. Me too."

Again I tried to sleep. It didn't work. In my mind were the lifeless eyes of a thousand faces, peering up from the sea; the wailing, the crying out. I wondered what exactly had happened to Corsberg. Had he died quickly?

I nudged Gee and motioned toward the steps leading out of the bilge to the open hatchway where a breeze billowed down in gusts, lessening the stench. We picked our way over bodies sprawled in every direction on blankets spread across the stinking straw. And we sat on the steel steps. "You know why we're in this mess?" Gee said.

"Japanese greed," I suggested.

"Not entirely. I think they're overcrowded. They need more real estate."

Many of us would live with this oversimplification until long after the war. Then we would discover that the Congress of the

United States had failed to appropriate funds for a stronger defense in the Far East, even after President Roosevelt and admirals of the Pacific fleet — Thomas C. Hart, for one — had warned that the Japanese were preparing for larger conquests. Who can say what Japan or Germany might have done had we beefed up our armed forces in the mid-thirties? Or if we had focused on what those countries really wanted and needed, finding the way to provide it, before they had gone beyond the point of no return.

What bothered us most was the subject we avoided altogether: the ship sailing alone, flying the Japanese flag, with no watertight compartments, no lifejackets, no chance if bombers struck.

All night we sat on the steps, dozing, listening to the pounding of giant screws churning the ocean, the creaking of steel against steel, the sounds of an ancient freighter moving on into darkness.

6

Dignity in a Bilge

I was up on deck for water the afternoon I saw the skyline of Singapore: a tall building glistening in the distance, which a British officer said was Bukit Timah. "It's called the mountain of tin," he added. We were heading toward the dock area and the huge warehouses, beyond which were yellow stucco houses with orange tile roofs. The buildings lay sparkling clean as though washed in a recent rain.

An eternity later we nudged the dock, and lines were thrown to the waiting dockhands. I stayed at the top of the hatchway, peering out, watching the Chinese coolies secure the lines to upright bitts then withdraw, staring up with ambivalence at the overhanging toilets.

There were only a few bombed-out warehouses along the docks, where dozens of dirty, busy cargo ships were tied. A Japanese navy officer full of self-importance stood talking to a Dutch captain, taking great pride in explaining the fall of Singapore. It was a great morale boost for the Japanese; devastating to the British, he chortled.

"Where are we being taken?" the Dutch officer asked. "What will become of us?"

"I do not know that, I am sorry to say."

We were taken out of the bilge and marched down the gangway to stand on the dock near a pier where Indonesians were being unloaded from another ship. The Indonesians coming down the gangplank were black from head to foot with coal dust. Granules of soot were in their eyes, ears, and nostrils; into the pores of their skin, deep into their sinuses. The Japanese were soon herding them onto waiting trucks. A Dutch doctor off the ship told Captain Fitzsimmons they were from Timor. The Indonesians were gentle people, he said, exposed for the first time to the reality of man's inhumanity. They thought when they were first invited on the ship to sail away to work that they were to be treated with dignity in the new "Greater East Asia Prosperity Sphere" program. But they were put into a bilge of coal dust, starved and kicked around, until they realized that they, too, were slaves of the Japanese. The Dutch doctor was kept with the prisoners from our ship. He watched the Indonesians go away in the trucks, feeling, he said, like a beautiful way of life was leaving, evaporating before his eyes. He was witnessing its passing, and he had a feeling it would never return.

In Camp Changi, a mile or so from downtown Singapore, 50,000 British soldiers were now imprisoned in their own garrison. This was to be the collecting point for all prisoners of war captured near the islands of the East Indies — all islands of the Malay Barrier, for that matter — and it was bulging at the seams.

It is unlikely that they could properly feed that many prisoners even if they wanted to and tried, a British officer told us. The needs of their own army and navy were enormous and obviously took precedence. Their supply lines were stretched too far, open to Allied bombers and submarines. Therefore, rice and basic food supplies had to come from the impoverished countries they occupied, and food crops in those countries were like wheat fields in Utah following a swarm of locusts.

Heat waves rose from the tile roofs of white stucco barracks, each building crammed with double the number of human bodies it was designed to accommodate. The British were supplementing what little food they got from the Japanese with tinned rations of their own, cached away inside the compound. But their hidden rations would soon be gone, and after that they would be no better off than the other prisoners. There was a critical shortage of fresh water. Water lines and drainage had been destroyed by bombs.

A white stucco-covered wall from six to twelve feet high, depending on the contour of the hilly ground, surrounded the camp. It would have been easy to scale had there been anywhere to go. By sheer numbers, the British could have overpowered the guards. But thousands of Japanese soldiers, armed to the teeth, were close by. Besides, at the time of surrender, the British had signed an agreement not to attempt escape.

Because of this "agreement," British officers could wear their rank on their collars and shoulders, and parade and preen in full uniform as though they still owned Singapore. Their enlisted men saluted them and otherwise took orders as if there had been no surrender.

Order came out of discipline, both matters of expedience in this environment. It would have been uncivilized to have allowed a relaxation of conduct where every man was out for himself. The British made life bearable and were smart for doing so. Scottish Highlanders played bagpipes at odd moments, though, often when least expected, jarring the nerves of those with undeveloped appreciations. "Entertainments" — prisoners singing, dancing, acting out plays — were often held in a stadium in which the British had once played rugby. And a Britisher could sneak out a tin of bully beef from time to time if his spirits sank too low.

We Americans could barely believe our eyes as we watched British soldiers stand at attention and salute their own officers, the officers actually prancing around expecting it. It was unbelievable that the British had apparently meant it when they promised they would not attempt escape. We had also signed such a document, but we knew we would run for it at the first opportunity. We understood the British officers' tradition of integrity — a promise is a promise, that sort of thing — and the British officers' tradition of being gentlemen above all, regardless of the circumstances. But we laughed about it among ourselves. Of course, none of us at the time knew what the British knew about the close proximity of armed Japanese in overwhelming numbers, and we knew not that the average Britisher, given the slightest opportunity to escape, would have led the pack.

The Dutch doctor, Henri Hekking, was placed in a barracks

where, gathered in one corner of the building, British, Australian, Dutch, and American officers were rehashing the fall of the East Indies, piecing together what pertinent details each could bring from a varied number of vantage points. I found him there, and I stood back, listening, while a British officer gave me a you-don't-belong-here fishy stare.

According to the conversation that ensued, at the time of the Java Sea battles it was known that the Japanese were on Sumatra, the island across Sunda Strait from Java; they were on Malaya to the northwest; to the north they were entrenched on Borneo and Celebes; and to the east they held Ambon and the Moluccas.

And it was known that if ABDA failed in the Java Sea battle, the Japanese would invade Java from the east and all of the East Indies would fold.

Dr. Hekking, Capt. Arch Fitzsimmons of the 131st Field Artillery, and a young British lieutenant who had been with the Royal Artillery were talking about the voyages of the two prison ships, the one from Timor, the other from Java. Henri told how Tjamplong was overrun, and how he had escaped being shot by caring for a Japanese *Kempeitai* officer, Major Tsuru. The *Kempeitai* was the Japanese elite intelligence force.

"What were you doing at the moment of capture?" the lieutenant wanted to know.

It sounded like a facetious question to me. "Trying to run," Hekking said.

"I say. Really!"

"Oh, yes. Pleading with a general to be allowed to leave with the rest of the troops. I am a doctor, not a fighter. My people had already gone to the hills, hoping to delay capture. We had torched the hospital, the barracks, the records —"

"And the bloody general wouldn't let you go?"

"That's right. He said I was to stay and take care of the wounded."

"But you are a doctor —"

"Yes, but there were no wounded. The British and the Australians had their own doctors. They didn't need me."

"Oh. So what did you do?"

"What I was ordered to do. I stayed in Tjamplong."

"And that's where Nippon got you?"

"Yes."

"Bad show," said the Englishman.

"Yes," said Hekking. He related in detail the occupation of Tjamplong, the feeble attempt of the Australians and Dutch to protect the island with antiaircraft guns along the Timor coast.

"Had you been on Timor very long?" Fitzsimmons asked.

"Not long in Timor. In the East Indies, many years. I went to Bergamo, Italy, in 1939, rather than take the one-year rest and relaxation leave to Holland I was entitled to take. I had an opportunity to study surgery with the famous Dr. Luciano at the University of Milan. I was in charge of the Surabaya Hospital at the time. I felt I needed the extra study in surgery. It was to have been a one-year study. But Hitler's troops went into Poland. Naturally, I was called back to the East Indies immediately. I served for a while in Tjimahi, Java, and then I was assigned to Tjamplong, Timor."

"Then you were in the Dutch Colonial Army, not the regular Dutch army," Captain Fitzsimmons said.

"Yes."

"There is a difference?"

"Well, the Colonial Army is trained to fight in the jungle, to survive in the jungle."

"How did you happen to be in the Colonial Army?" the lieutenant asked.

"I had gone to Holland when I was sixteen. My father worked in the East Indies for a Dutch company, and they wanted him back in The Hague for a period of retraining for a higher position. So I finished high school in Holland, and as a lad just out of high school I signed a contract to serve ten years with the Colonial Army in return for my medical education. You couldn't do that with the regular army. My father was not a wealthy man. It was the only way I could study medicine."

"And the Colonial Army was based in the colony — the East Indies," said the British lieutenant.

"Of course."

"I'll bet you would have preferred Holland to those islands," Fitzsimmons said.

"Oh, quite the contrary! I was born in Surabaya. Of Dutch parents, of course, but Java is my birthplace. To me, the islands of the East Indies are beautiful. I love Java and its people. I could hardly wait to get back. In fact, I promised my *oma*, my grandmother, I would come back, sooner or later, to offer medical service to the natives. It was special to me that I return, even though she had died. It was like going home."

"Oh," said Fitzsimmons, a little embarrassed. "Sorry. I didn't realize you would feel that way. I just didn't think."

Henri smiled. "It is all right. You could not have known."

"So you did go back to doctor the natives. Could you do that with the army?"

"Oh, yes, of course. It is important to the Netherlands government that the natives are cared for. It was important to my *oma*, and she cared for them, too, in a different way. She was an herbalist. She knew the jungle and the plant life that could be used for medicine. Every week she would go to the jungle for plants and herbs — many times I would go with her as a young lad — and every week thirty or forty natives would come and squat in the yard of her home and wait for her to give them a little bit of this and a little bit of that, perhaps a tea she had made. Or a poultice. It depended. And what she gave them, the herbs, the tea, sometimes just the things she would tell them, they were almost always helped, and they would go away feeling better and very grateful."

"Did she teach you what she knew about herbs?" Fitzsimmons asked.

"Yes, as much as I was willing to learn. She had a mystical quality few people understood. And of course I studied medicine at Leiden University in The Netherlands and tropical medicine with the army in Batavia, but no one ever taught me this special thing she knew. I eventually learned much about tropical diseases when I was on punishment duty for five years on Celebes."

"Punishment duty?" the Englishman exclaimed. "Five years? Good heavens, old boy! What on earth did you do?"

Henri looked at the lieutenant then looked away. "It was not very important," he said. "Perhaps another time."

We were in Camp Changi only one week. Again we were taken to the dock and put on a ship, its bilge also covered with straw and fresh cattle manure.

Dr. Hekking kept such a low profile few would remember seeing him. We laughed and poked fun at the situation. At one point I watched the puzzled look on his face as the marines, jammed together in one spot, were talking. It was small talk, meaningless, as usual. It was our way of covering up the apprehensions we felt. I know that now, looking back on it. If we were unusually nervous, or overly worried, nothing we said would reveal it. Except that we talked. And talked. This time the conversation was about a dancer we had known in Manila.

"Hey, Pluto, remember the Club Alabam?"

"Sure, Pinky. On top of the Great Eastern Hotel in Manila. Hot dog. What a place!"

"Remember that dancer, Felez, and how old Arnie was the only one to score?"

"Score? With Felez? Yer outta yer mind! All he did was take her home one night. He didn't score, not with Felez, he didn't!"

"Something weird with that woman."

"Mighty weird."

"Yeah! Just the kinda weird I like. That dance! Them hips, them laigs! Who-eeee, ha-a-ut dam!"

"No, I mean WEIRD weird. Askin' them questions about the ship. Where we'd just come in from. Where we wuz a-goin' next, stuff like that. Always them same questions."

"She was just bein' a mite friendly-lak, Pinky."

"Yeah, Smokey — probably workin' fer th' Japs!"

"Ah never told her nuthin'."

"Me neither!"

Silence for a few seconds. "Ole Arnie, if he tuk her out once't I bet he tuk her out twice't, and I'll betcha they wuz somethin' a-goin' on," said Smokey.

Bird Dog's voice: "Je-sus, I hope so! You're just jealous 'cause you never tuk her out."

"Well, how come he wuz the only one she'd go out with? Answer me that!"

"For one thing, he didn't hang around her, slobberin' down her bazoo like the rest of you knuckleheads. Now you take me, for instance."

"You take you, screw you."

"Don't you wish!"

"You didn't see me up there, hanging around that dame with my eyeballs a-poppin'."

"Yeah, Bird Dog. Big deal. So how come she never went out with you?"

"Because I never asked her, you birdbrain!"

"With windscoops for ears like yours? It wouldn't a-done you no good!"

"Oh, yeah? You ain't no ravin' beauty yourself, Pluto. Ears like a damn elephant . . ."

"Betcha ole Arnie laid her," said Pinky.

"Two bucks says he didn't."

"Yer on."

"How we gonna find out?"

"Ask him, you birdbrain!"

Later, Doc Hekking told us we reminded him of children at play, joking around about everything. We were in our teens and early twenties. He appreciated our youthfulness: he understood just enough of what was said to believe we were incapable of forming and expressing a single profound thought. After all, what had we read? Where had we been? What had we done? Had we ever experienced an opera? Did we even know what an opera was?

He sat in the straw, alternately trying to tolerate us and yet ignore us, speaking to no one.

7

Tales of Towana

I was surprised when Dr. Hekking nudged me. "Are you in charge of these men?"

"No," I told him. "I'm an enlisted man. Not an officer."

"I do not understand all they say."

"I could tell from the way you looked," I said. "What they're saying, well — I don't think you would want to know, sir. It's just our way of poking fun at one another. Anything for a laugh. You know?"

"I see. Well, I was sitting here, wondering if you Americans are ever serious."

I assumed he knew better than that. I didn't answer him.

"I myself, I am thinking of my wife and children," he said.

I knew he wanted to talk. I encouraged him.

He told me that his wife's name was May, and that he had a twelve-year-old son, Fred, and a nine-year-old daughter, Loukie. They were back on Timor, taken captive by the Japanese.

"Do you know where they took them?"

"Yes. It is a bad place, surrounded by barbed wire."

"You fear for their safety," I said.

He took a deep breath and nodded. "Yes, of course. It is

ironic. My wife's parents did not want the marriage to take place. They tried to break us up. They knew I would be taking her ten thousand miles away from Holland to Java. Her mother told my wife-to-be on the day of our wedding, 'Darling,' she said, 'there is still time to call it off.' What do you think of that! It was only a few hours before our marriage. I was never quite good enough for her parents, you see."

Dr. Hekking had a deep, resonant voice. Others were listening now, crowding even closer.

"You were married in Holland?" I asked.

"Yes. Near The Hague. Within days after I finished medical school at Leiden University I became a lieutenant, and we were married practically the next day. A few weeks after that we sailed for the East Indies."

"Did you have a choice about where they assigned you?" I asked.

"Oh, no. I had to serve in the Dutch East Indies."

"Then her parents couldn't blame you for taking her there."

There was a quiet composure, a dignity about this man, even as we sat in the bilge covered with cow dung.

"Are you a general practitioner?" someone asked.

"Yes. You could also say I am a specialist in tropical medicine."

"Did they teach that at the University of Leiden?"

"Some. At Leiden, however, it was mostly the kind of things all doctors are taught throughout the world. They taught me tropical medicine at Batavia Army Hospital. My grandmother taught me many things about the use of herbs for tropical illnesses and skin disorders. I also learned by actual experience in the Celebes."

"Oh," I said. "We saw Celebes from the vantage point of the USS *Houston.* We fought in Makassar Strait, between Celebes and Borneo. From the ship, that island looked like no human beings lived there. What was it really like?"

Hekking told us a revealing story about himself, reviewing a part of his life that had to have meant a great deal to him. To us it was a story of high adventure in the Celebes.

It was in June 1930, he said. How well he remembered the exhilaration of challenge — the prospect of doing something no other doctor had ever dared to try.

He and his wife May and his infant son Fred had just arrived on Celebes Island from Batavia to begin his punishment duty when he heard about the wild Towana natives of the mountain area. They needed medical help badly, and he was determined to go to them. He was to be in charge of the tiny "hospital" near the village of Kolonodale. Instead of feeling punished, he said he felt he was facing a future of exciting possibilities. He, May, and another Dutch couple, Lt. Adrie Nouwen and his wife, were the only two Dutch officer families near the Kolonodale garrison. Hekking had only a few patients, mainly because natives were afraid to come near the "civilized" hospital. He was determined to change that. Others had told him that the loneliness of the place would be the worst part of the punishment. But he knew he would never be lonely, as long as there were people in need of help.

A German minister, Pastor Riedell, was the one who had told him about the Towana, describing the awful sores they had on their bodies. The mountains where they lived were north of the Gulf of Tomori in the shortest of the four arms of Celebes Island. Henri would need a guide to help him find them and to help him with their language, Riedell advised. Riedell also had a warning: the Towana were dangerous.

Henri said he went to Radja Razak in the nearby village of Boengkoe to ask for help in finding a guide. Though fierce-looking in his warlike attire, the Islamic Radja Razak was a kind, attentive man. He sat in his little shack which served as a reception hall, listening patiently, impressed with the purpose of Henri's proposed mission. "To get to the Towana you will have to take a boat from Kolonodale to Morowali, then walk up the treacherous mountainside on foot. You will need horses to carry supplies," Razak said. "It will be easier to find a guide to search for babirusa, the ferocious wild hog, than to find a man who will search for Towana."

"What is there to fear?" Henri asked.

"Blowguns. Poison arrows. Towana kill people who come to their mountains!"

Henri said he had no reason to doubt the radja. But it

would be easy to prepare a way to deal with poison arrows. "I will see that no harm comes to the guide who goes with me," he said. "When I give him my antidote, the arrows will no longer be poison."

Radja Razak was a patient man. So were his aides, sitting passively beside him. "Why have you no fear?" the radja asked. "White skin will not protect you. Towana kill you same as others. Towana respect no man who intrudes, white or brown."

"I am a very lucky fellow," Henri said. "I have an honest face. I smile a lot. The Towana will know I'm there to help. They will not harm me."

"The last man who went up there was trying to count them. Maybe he smiled also. I do not know. They filled him with poison arrows. He never come back."

Henri laughed. "I am not a census taker. I am a doctor."

They sat in silence staring at each other, the faces of the aides like carved statues.

"You are a persistent man," the radja said.

"If you cannot help me, I will go alone," Henri replied, nodding toward the mountains.

"You are also very stubborn."

"Yes."

The radja wagged his head. "There is one man who knows how to find Towana. He speaks their language. He is also very stubborn. I will talk to him. Perhaps I can persuade him to go with you. His name is Abdul."

"Where is this Abdul?"

"In jail. For murder."

The jail was a filthy place about the size of a two-car garage. Of white stucco sides and dirt floor, it was surrounded by a high concrete wall with broken glass embedded along the top.

Abdul was dirty, ragged, and in need of a shave. Looking at him through bars, it was difficult to know how old he was. As Dr. Hekking and the radja drew close, he got up from his mat, scratched his crotch, and grinned out at them. He stood erect, clinging to the bars. He was not an idiot. There was just the trace of dignity about him.

Radja Razak had the jailer open the door so Henri could go inside. The cell stank of body odor. Razak and the jailer stood back, leaving Henri alone with Abdul.

Henri spoke in Malayan. "I would like you to make a two-week journey with me."

Abdul displayed a row of brown, rotted teeth. "A journey? To where?"

"To the mountains to find Towana."

Abdul's eyes widened, then narrowed. He looked away. "I do not wish such a journey."

"What do you know about Towana?" Henri asked.

"Enough." He shook his head. "I cannot go. I wish to stay alive."

"You have two choices," Henri said. "Either you lead me to the Towana and become a free man afterwards, or the radja will keep you in jail. If you do not believe me, ask him. He is standing right over there."

Abdul drew back a little, as if Henri had struck him — as if others had struck him also, many times. He appeared to be thinking it over. "I will remain in jail. It is better than the slow death of poison."

"I have an antidote — medicine I can inject. The poison of arrows will mean nothing."

Abdul looked dubious. "Will it stop the poison of snakes?"

"Oh, yes, of course."

Henri said he had heard that it took twenty minutes for poison from the arrows to kill a person once it got into the bloodstream, and he knew that within much less time than that he could inject shots of pain killer and Adrenalin around the arrow hole, then use a scalpel to remove flesh in the immediate area where the arrow had penetrated. A small bandage to cover the wound would be all there was to it. The same procedure would work for snakebites.

"How about the leech?" Abdul asked. "Do you have medicine to kill the leech?"

"Oh, yes. Tobacco."

Henri carried tobacco to ward off the bloodsucking annelid worm, which he, too, feared. They were everywhere in the jungles of Celebes. One could not feel them when they first attached themselves to the back, or legs, or soft flesh of the side. As they sucked blood from their victim, they could sometimes become as large as a fist before they were noticed. Tobacco juice on the arms, legs, and back discouraged them.

The Nouwens were visiting the Hekkings that night, and before Adrie had a chance to ask too many questions, Henri took him outside.

"That man you have out back," Adrie said. "That's Abdul, the murderer!"

"Of course. I know."

"What is he doing here?"

"He's to be my guide."

"Henri, you're not —!"

"Oh, yes. First thing in the morning. We'll be back in two weeks."

"Two weeks! And you haven't told May?"

"Of course I've told her. She knows we're going to the mountains to visit the poor, sick Towana. She knows when we plan to return. She isn't worried."

"She isn't worried because she doesn't know about those people! She doesn't know about Abdul!"

"That's right," said Henri. "And you must not tell her."

Dr. Hekking, an aide named Lapakiri, and Abdul went by boat across the fjord. It took two hours. They picked up two horses from villagers near the foothills, secured their supplies on the horses' backs, then the three men walked and led the horses up through the underbrush along the side of the mountain.

They had walked for many hours in silence.

"They have been here," Abdul said, fear etched on his face.

"Don't worry. You have the antidote in your blood. If

they shoot you, nothing will happen. We'll just pull the arrow out and throw it away."

They stopped on an outcropping of rock to have lunch — pieces of chicken and handfuls of rice wrapped in fresh green banana leaves.

Abdul smacked his lips and licked his fingers. "It is a good meal. I hope it is not the last."

"What language do they speak?" Henri asked.

"A language of the devil," Abdul said. "I came near their campfire one night when I was young and very daring and very stupid. I heard them talking. They had caught one of their own men in an act of adultery. They were preparing to eat him alive. They cut him a little at first so he would bleed well while he was alive. They drained some of his blood, and the parents of the offended wife drank the blood while it was still warm. The men ate the heels of his feet while he was screaming. You see, they consider the heels a delicacy. It was an awful sight. The worst sight I ever saw. I sneaked away in the night."

Henri knew Abdul's story was fabricated and totally preposterous, but he wouldn't challenge it, not yet. "What language did they speak?" he asked.

"It is a Baree dialect."

They had finished eating and were about to resume their journey. It suddenly became quiet.

"They are close," said Abdul, rolling his eyes. "They are watching."

"How do you know?" Henri asked.

"Listen," Abdul whispered.

Henri listened. "I hear nothing."

"That," Abdul hissed, "is how you know."

An hour or so later the three men reached the peak of the mountain and stopped in a large clearing. They could tell from footprints that human beings had been there.

"I am very tired. We will build a lean-to and rest," Henri said.

Abdul believed they should keep moving, but he tethered the horses and they worked in silence, building the lean-to with limbs cut from trees at the edge of the clearing, trimmed with a hatchet. They used poles lashed together with bark, held at a slant, tied to upright poles driven in the ground. They covered the top with leaves.

As soon as the shelter was ready, Abdul set up a cot and Henri stretched out in the shade. He lay on his back. "Wake me in thirty minutes," he said.

"How can you sleep when you know they are watching?" Abdul wondered.

"I am here to help them," Henri said. "I have an honest look. They will know."

The sound came from a long way off, like an approaching storm. Slowly, it gathered in volume, as the sound of a rain grows moving across a jungle, coming closer. And then someone was nudging him, shaking him. "Awaken!" Abdul was saying. "They are upon us!"

Henri looked up at a crowd of black people, all eyeing him; women naked from the waist up, men nude except for tiny pieces of bark. Naked children peered around the sides of women's legs. There was no antagonism or fear; just hundreds of eyes filled with curiosity.

They were talking to one another, buzzing like bees. When the doctor raised up on his cot, the buzzing abruptly stopped. They drew back eight or ten feet. No one appeared to have weapons.

Henri grinned and nodded at a little boy who had not pulled away. The boy smiled, holding fingers to his mouth. He stood there. A woman watched and a smile twinkled in her eyes.

Getting slowly to his feet, Henri gently took the boy by the hand. He spoke in Malaysian. "Are there any sick people here?"

From the puzzled looks he knew they didn't understand. Abdul asked questions in a language they did understand. One of the black men said something, and the others appeared to nod assent.

"Well, what did he say?" Henri asked.

"I told them you were a white medicine man, and that you only wanted to help them. They understood." Abdul grinned. "I don't think they'll kill us until they're ready for dinner."

"You think they're cannibals?"

"No. Unless they catch you touching one of the wives. Then you can watch them drink your blood."

Henri was looking at the red rash around one of the women's breasts. Many of the women had sores around the nipples that looked like ripe strawberries. Some were nursing babies, and the babies had the identical kinds of sores around their mouths. It was framboesia — he had seen it in Java, but never as big and as angry-looking as this. It had to be terribly painful. Some of the sores were as large as his hand.

He drew close to a woman and her baby, smiling, nodding reassurance, ignoring the smell of rotted flesh. He made a great to-do about the baby, taking it gently in his arms, laying it down on his cot. Hundreds of eyes watched his every move. He made a quick examination of the infant, listening with the stethescope to breathing and heartbeat, feeling for internal abnormalities by gently pushing his fingers along the stomach and abdomen. The baby appeared to be healthy, except for the framboesia sores around the mouth.

Framboesia — also called "yaws" — was a contagious skin disease having many analogies with syphilis. Although it was not the same thing, it was ultimately as dangerous if allowed to go untreated. Henri knew that with a microscope he would have seen the same spirochete, or spirally undulating microorganisms like tiny corkscrews, that are characteristic of syphilis. Yet here the curves of each spiral would be longer.

Eventually, sulfa would be used for such things as yaws and syphilis. A German bacteriologist, Gerhard Domagk, was doing research at the time which would ultimately have a far-reaching impact. Meanwhile, Henri would try Neo-Salversan, or arsphenamine (a light yellow oxidizable hygroscopic powder normally used as a specific remedy for syphilis). He would use it on both women and children when they became relaxed with him.

He returned the baby to its mother then inspected the sores on the mother's breasts, clucking his tongue in sympathy, pointing to the baby's mouth then to the sores around her nipples. "Abdul, tell this woman I will try to make these sores go away," he said.

Abdul spoke to the woman. She looked at Henri as though he were a god.

There were numerous skin diseases, particularly among the adults. Some had dried skin like elephant hide. Some had pustules and various kinds of open and infected sores. Many were of a fungus variety. There was something else that bothered Henri: men squatting and sitting on the ground having difficulty keeping their eyes open. It was still an hour before sundown. Either they were tired from some kind of abnormal exertion, or sick.

He had Lapakiri bring forth a spray gun from one of the saddle bags, and asked him to fill it from a jug of salicylic acid, a common antiseptic that inhibits and sometimes stops entirely the growth of fungi. The spray gun was the hand-pump type normally used in spraying insect poison. He sprayed some of the acid on his own arm to show that it was harmless. He then held his arm up so the Towanas could watch as it turned white. He had Abdul tell them that the spray was to help cure the sores on their bodies.

A woman came forward, pointing to the sores on her arms. Henri sprayed them. The acid cooled the skin, soothing the pain immediately. The woman laughed as her arm turned white. She talked excitely to the crowd. Other women emerged, and soon a line formed. Lapakiri was careful not to spray the acid on open sores. But he was busy spraying the women's arms, legs, backs, and shoulders until the sun went down and darkness fell.

Henri told Abdul to light a lantern. He watched him do it, and seconds later when he turned around the Towana were gone.

It was totally silent — as though the Towana had never been there and had never existed.

"They'll be back," Abdul said. "Tomorrow. They'll bring the rest of the tribe. You'll see."

Abdul was right.

The whinnying of a horse awakened them. When they arose and looked out, the entire clearing was covered with

Towana — as many as a hundred, squatting on haunches, waiting in silence. The horse they had heard was their own. These people had come by foot. How far, there was no way of knowing. How long they had been there, or how long they would have remained silent to avoid awakening them, they would never know.

The Towana had brought special gifts of food for Henri, Lapakiri, and Abdul — stalks of sugar cane and taro roots — and had laid them down in front of the lean-to.

Henri spent most of the day giving inoculations of Neo-Salversan to the women and infants who had framboesia. In many of the small babies it was almost impossible to find an artery for the needle, and Lapakiri had to help hold them as they screamed. But both he and Abdul had apparently won their confidence. None of the women held back; none of the men acted as though they objected. They could not expect instant results, Henri told them. He would be back in ten days, and by then the framboesia would be under control. They didn't understand "ten days." Abdul had to do a drawing in the dirt with a stick, showing the fullness of the moon now and what the moon would be like when they returned almost two weeks later. When they finally understood, word swept through the crowd like the whisper of wind, the sound of hope.

They shared their food at noon, and by then the Towana men were in a playful mood. The blowguns appeared. Both men and boys engaged in target practice, shooting arrows at a tree with incredible accuracy. It was all in fun. Henri was encouraged to take a turn. He did, missing the tree entirely, to the loud laughter of everyone. Where were the guns before? Henri asked. Hidden in the bush, near at hand, not to be shown for fear the white man would be frightened away.

Some of the men did not participate in the fun. They squatted on their haunches, staring into space, or sat with their backs against trees, asleep. Henri examined one of the men who had been asleep. He found nothing out of the ordinary. But he knew something was wrong with this man and the others who fell asleep so easily in broad daylight. He thought at first it might possibly be a form of filariasis.

People with this disease looked emaciated and bloodless, and often the lymph glands in their groins were swollen. To make a positive diagnosis, blood samples had to be made at night because the germs of *filariasis nocturna* remain in the spleen during the day. That night he took numerous blood samples, placing ten drops to a slide, allowing the slides to dry, then packing them for the long trip back to Kolonodale Hospital.

On the way back by the village of Morowali several days later, Henri was walking, leading his horse in front, feeling happy and optimistic about future trips to the sick people in his area, particularly the Towana. He couldn't understand the great sadness that had come over Abdul. He asked him why he was so silent.

"I didn't steal a single horse, and yet I enjoyed myself," Abdul said.

Henri laughed. "That makes you sad?"

"In a way. I am no longer myself."

"Is that so bad?"

"It is painful. First time in my life I am a good man. Now, I must say goodbye to you, Doctor, my friend."

Henri stopped and looked back.

"Stay in the village, Abdul. Make yourself available. There is important work to do. I need you to help."

"You mean that?"

"Of course!"

Abdul grinned with a look of hope, tentatively, as though he dared not believe Henri. The doctor nodded reassuringly. "I saw how you love children. I know you want to help. There is a way. You can serve as guide on future trips."

Happiness shone in Abdul's eyes.

The blood samples provided a startling revelation. Practically the entire Towana population from the age of two months up was infected with micro-filaria (Brugia Malayi) — slender nematode worms, microscopic in size, parasitic in blood and body tissues. No wonder the men and many of the women were so tired and listless. It wasn't laziness, as Nouwen and many of the villagers thought. It was worms!

Some time passed before Henri and Abdul could return to the mountain area of the Towana. When they finally did make the trip, a number of the young natives met them in the foothills and gleefully accompanied them the rest of the way. It was a happy reunion. The Neo-Salversan had worked miracles with the women and infants: there was hardly a trace of framboesia. However, no treatment for filariasis existed. It would be ten years before an effective method was available even for testing.

There were many myths about the Towana, almost all the figment of someone's imagination. Henri could find no confirmation of the stories about Towana natives torturing people. Nor was the story accurate that Towana did not communicate with other "wild" tribes, much less with "civilized" villagers or with the Dutch.

Natives of the islands, including Towana, had uncanny ways of communicating. In Celebes the different tribes passed messages back and forth by way of a rapid system the Dutch called "the jungle express." Whether it was done with drums or by imitations of bird or animal calls, or through a combination of these, neither Henri nor Abdul was ever certain, even after spending so much time with them. What they did discover was the fact that many natives on the island of Celebes now knew that Dr. Hekking had brought dramatic help to the Towana.

Over the next several months, that information reached as far south as Bandoeng, Java, headquarters of the Colonial Army — not by jungle express, but through the routine monthly reports both Henri and Nouwen had to write and send in. It was Nouwen's report that spelled out the reaction of the natives to Henri. "They think of him as their great saviour," Nouwen reported. "They call him 'Bapak' (or father). There is no way of telling how many lives he has saved."

"Well, that is how I came to learn so much more about tropical medicines than I knew before," Doc said. "You see, I had my own little herb garden on Celebes, too, almost identical to the one my *oma* had."

"You said you were there for punishment duty?"

"Yes, but that is another story. It is not important."

I thought of urging him to tell it. But I sensed it was time to let him stop.

"Perhaps sometime you'll tell us," I said.

"Oh, yes. Sometime."

I didn't know what to make of Doc's story. I think I was caught up in the personality of Doc himself as much as I was in his story. Little did we know that later on we would attach such a life-and-death meaning to herbs.

It was only a two-day trip. The night was late when we walked down the gangplank onto the dock — where, we had no idea. We were led in almost total darkness down a narrow cobblestone street to a large wrought-iron gate. We thought it was a gate to a prison. Someone thought we were in Rangoon. Guards opened the gate, waved their lanterns, and told us to find a place anywhere inside to lie down. We stood like dazed cattle, staring into the darkness as the gate clanged shut behind us. There was not enough light to be selective, only enough to make out across the fence the outlines of a huge pagoda with lengths of glass hanging down inside the dome. We could barely make out the shape of a long building, and Dr. Hekking and I and several Americans found a door to it and stepped inside into even greater darkness. We unrolled our mats and blankets and stretched out on a slab of concrete, pulling a blanket up under our chins.

The wind came up during the night, causing the strips of glass to set up a loud clanging noise inside the pagoda; and dogs yowled with each round of clanging.

"Welcome to Moulmein, Burma, folks," James Gee announced.

"Oh, yeah? How do you know it's Moulmein, smart-ass?" asked Pluto Aust.

"Ever hear of Rudyard Kipling?"

"Nope."

"He wrote a poem called 'Road To Mandalay.' It was made into a song."

"So? What's that got to do with Moulmein?"

A tired voice: "Would you two guys just please button it up?"

"I know the song," said Fred Quick. "It goes —"

"Oh, fer christsake!"

Fred sang: "By the old Moulmein pagoda, lookin' lazy to the sea, there's a Burma girl a-waitin', and she's waitin' there for me."

Fred had a fantastic baritone voice. No one ever tried to stop him from singing.

We were awakened by bright sunlight shining in our eyes. When we sat up and looked around, the people sitting a dozen feet away gaped and shrank back into blankets, frightened looks in their eyes. Some who had not awakened lay without blankets. Their faces were disfigured. Some had no arms, no legs or hands.

We got up and looked around. We were scattered about on the grounds, some inside the shelter, still asleep near the disfigured ones. Finally, we were told: we were in a place occupied by lepers.

8

Assignment in Burma

October 30, 1942

We were taken inland from Moulmein by train that morning, riding on flatcars, the steam locomotive chugging its way past scenery that might have been beautiful at another time. But we were hungry and apprehensive, and subdued by an overpowering jungle that nudged the roadbed on each side, intensifying with each passing mile.

After a few hours the train stopped at the tiny village of Thanbyuzayat, and guards brandishing rifles told us to get off.

They herded us past the curious villagers and onto an open field. We still had no idea about what was in store for us. We took each moment as it came. There was no way to know that, later on, even the word Thanbyuzayat would have the connotation of death.

Guards were burning brush around the edge of the clearing, and smoke from the huge bonfires drifted into our nostrils. We were lined up in front of a raised wooden platform, counted, and ordered to stay at attention. A Japanese colonel — we learned later that his name was Nagatomo — and a British lieutenant walked up on the platform to look down upon us. We were told to stand at ease, and the colonel spoke in a loud voice as the British lieutenant interpreted: we were here to build a railroad for the Japanese army, and this was the starting point. It would extend from here 262 miles through the jungle south by southeast to Bangkok. We would complete it in twelve months.

Nothing was said by the Japanese, but our officers knew that it was critical that they have this rail link to Bangkok. As of now, supply ships from Japan sailed 5,000 miles across the open expanse of the Pacific, then across the South China Sea, around the Malayan Peninsula, north by northwest across the Indian Ocean, and finally over the Bay of Bengal to Rangoon — exposed the entire distance to Allied submarines and aircraft. And even when the cargo arrived in Rangoon there was no way to transfer it southward through the jungle except on the backs of human carriers. The new railroad would eliminate half the problem. Supplies could be off-loaded in Saigon, transferred up the Mekong River to Bangkok, then transported overland by rail directly to front lines in Burma.

The project was not described in this manner by Colonel Nagatomo, the railroad commanding officer. Instead, he presented the job as a reason our lives were spared; as an opportunity for us to redeem ourselves for our foolish attempt to defeat the "mighty Dia Nippon Gun." As he talked, guards ringed the sweltering field. Cloth around the backs of their caps hung motionless. Nagatomo's uniform was saturated with sweat.

Thousands more would be brought here to hear this speech during the next few weeks:

"You are only a few remaining skeletons of those who tried to defeat Japan . . . You are pitiful victims. You have no fighting power left . . . but the Imperial thoughts are inestimable and the Imperial favors are infinite that your lives have been spared for a great work . . . and you should weep with gratitude . . ."

The jibberish droned on, given meaning by the lieutenant, words and phrases sealing our fate. "We will complete it in one year even if we must do it over the white man's body. If a man is trying to escape this work, he shall see big jungles toward the east which are impossible to penetrate. Toward the west he shall see boundless ocean, and, above all, in the main points of the north and south our Nippon armies are guarding. If a man here tries to escape we will make him face the extreme penalty."

We stared out at the matted trees, the ferns, the vines and undergrowth, looking for signs of hope and finding none. Not one leaf was stirring. We studied each other's faces for proof we were hearing the same things, hoping for signs of hope, but seeing none.

Surely this was the acting out of an ill-conceived play, Captain Fitzsimmons observed. Did the Japanese know what the jungles were like? He had read just enough about railroads to know that the British were the first to build them, the first to study the feasibility of a railroad across Burma to Bangkok — a project they had rejected because of the estimated cost in human lives and British pounds. Abnormally heavy rains in monsoon season, uneven terrain, flooding, and an ungodly jungle rampant with disease were among the major obstacles the British foresaw.

But it would cost the Japanese very little. It might cost us our lives.

At last we were allowed to sit and rest on the open field. Sergeant Dupler slumped over and was carried inside the temporary "hospital," a bamboo and atap structure the size of a small gymnasium.

"Can we do it?" one Australian asked another.

"Build the bloody railroad? You askin' me? Blimey, mate. How should I know?"

Henri joined several British, American, and Australian doctors who were permitted to stand at the edge of the clearing. A Dr. Wiggins the others deferred to was talking to a Japanese officer, Dr. Sagara, about the shortage of doctors and medical supplies. The British interpreter came to help Sagara. Some camps would be without doctors altogether but would share medical services with those that did have doctors, Sagara said through the interpreter. He would do the best he could to get medical supplies, but they had to understand that a war was on and the Japanese army got first crack at both food and medicine.

Wiggins shook hands with Henri, eyeing the stethescope. "Captain Hekking, is it? Doctor, eh? Do you have your papers?"

"No. My hospital was overrun. My wife — I think my wife was able to hang on to my certificate. I hope so. I'm not certain."

"Hmm," Wiggins said, pursing his lips. "Too bad. But I'm sure some of your Dutch friends are around to vouch for you."

Henri studied the sea of faces on the open field. "I hope so," he said.

"Of course, we British and Australians had the good or bad

fortune, whichever, to be captured intact, so to speak. At least we jolly well know one another. Too well, I'm afraid.'' He laughed.

"Are you implying I need a certificate to practice medicine in ... in a prisoner-of-war camp?''

"No, no of course not, my dear chap! But of course it is just as important that you be a certified doctor here as anywhere else where you practice, eh, wot? But your performance will be proof enough, I dare say, won't it?''

The base hospital would be in one of the long bamboo buildings soon to be built on this open field. Those already in need of medical attention would remain here in temporary quarters — a bamboo shack — until they were well enough to join their units. Worst cases would be sent here from the work camps, Wiggins explained to Henri and the other doctors.

Lieutenant Sagara bowed politely, grinning, showing his gold teeth, sucking his gums. Apparently, he was just out of medical school. It was obvious that if he knew anything about tropical medicine he wasn't saying.

Wiggins was holding forth again. Sitting on the ground within hearing distance was an American soldier with a bandaged leg, listening intently as the British doctor described his numerous medical successes.

"I've developed a system for amputating limbs," Wiggins said. "I can cut off a leg and cauterize it in less than eight minutes. With a couple of chaps holding, of course. What do you think of that?''

"I do not believe in amputations," Henri said.

Wiggins snorted and drew back.

Henri explained. "Once a person loses a limb he never gets it back. My policy is to avoid taking it in the first place.''

"Come, now," Wiggins scoffed. "No one takes a limb unless he has to. What do you do when gangrene develops?''

"Scrape," said Henri.

"Scrape! I say!''

Henri saw the look on the young American's face. He stopped talking, took Wiggins by the shoulder, and led him back where the American couldn't hear.

He described his scraping process and his method of making bandages, stressing the need to keep open sores and scraped areas

free of bandages which restricted access to air, vital to the process
of healing.

Wiggins listened, obviously unimpressed. "Barbaric!" he
muttered.

"So are amputations," Henri retorted.

"Who is that doctor?" the American soldier asked me.

"He's Dr. Hekking," I said. I introduced myself to the soldier.
His name was Glen Self. "Glen," I said, "my bet is that Hekking
knows more about tropical ulcers than all of the rest of those doctors put together."

Each work camp along the railroad was designated by a number indicating its distance from base headquarters. The 190 Americans and 590 Australians with whom we had come from Singapore
were told we would be moving out right away to the camp at Kilo
40. The highest-ranking prisoner at Kilo 40 was Australian Col.
C. M. Black. The American was Capt. Arch L. Fitzsimmons,
whom Henri remembered from Singapore.

Henri asked Colonel Nagatomo if he were supposed to stay in
Thanbyuzayat or go with Colonel Black's force, the outfit he had
arrived with from Singapore. In the confusion Nagatomo mumbled
something like "Ush," motioning toward the Americans.

There were not enough trucks to transport the entire group in
one trip. As soon as the available trucks were loaded and had
pulled out, the remaining prisoners — Americans — were made to
walk along the jungle road. It was a long, grueling, depressing hike,
moving into the tangled jungle. But we set a spirited pace and
maintained it.

"Slug" Wright, the soldier who had been decked by the guard
for taking water from a steam pipe, jogged alongside Henri. The
long-legged American marines of the *Houston* were setting the pace,
causing Slug to have to run, and Henri wondered why. "You a doctor?" Slug asked, gasping for air, eyeing the stethescope.

It was like asking if water was wet. "Yes," Henri grunted.

"I'm a medic," Slug panted, grinning from ear to ear.

"Yes?"

"You don't know what a medic is? A medic's like a corpsman."

"Yes?"

"You don't know what a corpsman is?"

"No. Is corpsman like pharmacist?"

"No, a pharmacist is a guy who works in a drug store, pushing pills and stuff."

"Stuff? What is 'stuff'?"

"Anything," Slug said. "Sodapop. Ice cream. Shakes. Got it?"

"What you mean, anything?"

"Stuff."

It sounded like the who's-on-first routine. Those of us listening thought it was funny. It was good to laugh.

Henri eyed the little guy taking two steps to his one. "You are crazy. All you Americans, crazy!"

"Come on, Doc. I was just kiddin'."

Henri didn't know what "kiddin' " meant, either. "Why are we walking like this? Why such hurry?"

"Look at them Nips, Doc! They're plumb tuckered out. That's why we're walkin' so fast — jist to prove we're stronger'n they are, and to let 'em know they ain't gonna get us down!"

"Is it so important to prove something?"

"Sure. That's the American way."

We walked into a profusion of jungle so thick the sun didn't shine. There was almost no low-growing vegetation. Even the vines looked skinny and sick compared to the large ones filled with water in the East Indies. Every limb and bush had a picked-over look, as though too many animals, Homo sapiens included, had taken too much over too long a period of time, and now it was barren.

"What I am," said Slug Wright, "is like a medical assistant."

"Oh, I see! 'Medical assistant!' Why did you not say that in the first place? Why do you not speak English?"

"Because I'm Texan. In Texas we don't speak English. We don't even speak American. We speak Texan." Slug laughed.

Henri failed to see the humor.

"We got another guy who's a real first-rate corpsman," Slug said. "Name's Hanley. Doc Hanley, we call him. Off th' *Houston*. You'll want him to help you fer sure, Doc."

"Yes," said Henri. "Of course. I will need much help."

An American catching up to them was carrying a gunny sack with something clonking around inside. Henri did a double-take.

He and Slug exchanged glances. "What is that?" Henri asked.

"That sounds to me like tin cans, bottles, stuff like that. You gotta know who he is to appreciate him," Slug said. "He's Jim McCone. Packrat, we call him. Best we be downright friendly with him. One day, you and I may need some of his junk."

On we trudged, into the illogic of twisted vines and gnarled roots. There were no sounds except the scattering of animals and the flapping of frightened birds; no human voices, not even the yells of guards. It was as though each man had locked himself into his own deep depression.

Suddenly, one of the prisoners began to sing, a voice filled with energy, as though its owner could march for a hundred more miles.

"From the Halls of Monte-zuuuu-a-ma to the shores of Trip-o-leeee . . ."

Another man joined him — then another, and another, and soon we were all singing the "Marine Corps Hymn." Then we shifted to other tunes.

"My Bonnie lies over the ocean. My Bonnie lies over the sea. My Bonnie lies over the ocean; Oh, bring back my Bonnie to meeeeee!"

Who cared if we sang off key, or if we didn't know the words? The vines were not so tangled anymore, the shadowy trees were less intimidating, and even the birds circling high and away could join the songs of the free spirit, of blind belief. Songs tingled along the spine, and down the legs, all the way to the toes: songs of the need to live — the will to live — sung at the tops of our lungs.

"You Americans, crazy guys," Hekking smiled.

The songs came to an abrupt halt as we stopped at the gate of a dreary camp: a clearing fenced in with barbed wire, steam rising around seven buildings built with half-green bamboo poles and roofed over with fresh green atap leaves. In time, the bamboo would dry and yellow and turn brown and there would be less steam and no one would know the difference or care, Henri said. "This is terrible place."

There were no doors or screens or mosquito netting. Through the center, running the length of each building, was a dirt aisle. On each side were long, continuous shelves built knee-high, eight feet deep. We would sleep on these shelves made of one-inch-thick bamboo poles built on top of thicker cross members. We would sleep on them, and each morning we would look like something from the grill.

Behind each building were slit trenches a foot wide and two feet deep, huge blue flies already there, buzzing expectantly. A creek sliced across a back corner of the clearing. Muddy water could be carried from there and boiled in one of the three large cauldrons in an open "kitchen," a shelter consisting of a slanted atap roof held aloft on bamboo poles driven a foot or two into the ground.

Doc inspected the kitchen. He found only dirty rice and a few vegetables.

He went directly to the Japanese camp commander who stood near the gate, with arms folded across his chest as he watched prisoners file into the barracks.

"I am Dr. Hekking, your camp physician," he announced, managing a kind of salute.

"Major Yamada," the commander said, returning the salute, barely nodding his head. He was a tough-looking, imposing man.

"I wish to speak about food," Henri said.

"*Horyo* prepare food," Yamada grunted.

"The men will need meat," Doc said.

"No meat. Later, Nippon kill water buffalo. Boom-boom. Understand-kah?"

"The men must have meat and citrus — fruit, any kind of fruit," Henri said.

"Fruit? *Watachiwa wakaranai*," Yamada said.

Doc acted as though he were peeling a banana; then as though he were peeling a grapefruit. "Fruit," he kept repeating.

Yamada shook his head. "No fruit," he said.

"As a doctor, I must warn you that if you do not provide protein and citrus these men will soon become sick, and if they become sick, how do you build a railroad?"

Yamada's frown changed to a malicious grin. "You warn me, Captain?"

"Yes. I warn you."

Doc may not have seen the slight movement of Yamada's shoulder. But he had to have felt the blow on his cheek. He was reeling backward, trying to regain his balance, holding his face. It had happened so fast he probably wasn't sure what hit him.

"You do not warn me, Doctor! I warn you! You will speak no more of food!"

Doc backed away.

Minutes later, Yamada ordered roll call. He gave a speech covering points Nagatomo had neglected. Prisoners were worthless driftwood washed ashore on the tide, he said. In Japan, one who surrendered to the enemy was worse than worthless: he was dead, for all practical purposes. He could never go home again, members of his family were disgraced, his offspring would suffer for many generations. But we were lucky: the railroad gave us the opportunity to redeem ourselves. If we worked hard and completed the railroad on schedule, we might even deserve to live.

Yamada said his ambition was to accomplish more with his segment of the railroad than any other commander along the railroad. In what seemed like the middle of his speech, an American's voice sang out — a beautiful baritone, challenging the Japanese lieutenant, mocking everything he stood for:

> *"God bless Ah-mer-i-ca,*
> *Land that I luvvvvvvvv —*
> *Stand beside her, and guide her,*
> *Through th' night with a light*
> *From a-bove —"*

Yamada's face grew pale then reddened. His eyes searched the rows of men until he located the singer. "Stop!" he shouted.

He motioned to two guards who ran into ranks and grabbed the man by the arms. They yanked him out to stand in front of Yamada.

"Nanda?" Yamada roared.

The man shrugged. He said nothing.

"Nanda!" Yamada shouted, slapping the man in the face.

"He doesn't speak Japanese," Captain Fitzsimmons said.

"Name!" Yamada yelled. "What is name?"

"Quick, Fred B., Junior. Private, United States Marines. Serial Number 284,977 —"

"Louder!"

Fred Quick started all over again. Meanwhile, the guards tied his hands behind his back. They found a bamboo pole about five feet long and three inches in diameter. Each time he gave his name, rank, and serial number a guard whacked him over the head with the pole. His nose began to bleed. He would not cry out nor make a sound, except to repeat: "Quick, Fred B., Junior. United States Marines. Serial Number —" And — whack!

They struck him. They held the pole behind his knees and made him squat. This cut off the circulation from his knees down.

They found a second pole and raised it above his head.

"Sing!" Yamada ordered.

He refused.

Down came the pole, and blood spurted from Quick's mouth. His eyes glazed over.

"Stop!" Henri yelled. "You will kill that man!"

Pain shot across Henri's back. As he doubled over he realized a guard had struck him from behind with a rifle butt.

"Sing!" Yamada shouted, and the pole came down again.

"God . . . bless . . ." The words trailed off.

They beat him with the pole until he pitched forward, unconscious.

After the guards and Yamada left, Doc followed four of us who carried Quick inside one of the buildings. We laid him out along the edge of the bamboo shelf so Henri could check him over. Quick was a rugged man, six feet tall. Henri had heard him sing once, in Singapore in one of the "entertainments." Quick had been a professional entertainer in a night club at the edge of Kansas City before he joined the marines.

"Is he gonna live?" someone asked.

"Oh, yes," Doc said, inspecting the deep gash on the back of Quick's head. "I would sew this up, if I had some way to disinfect it. If I had a suture and thread."

"I can get some boiled water," Gee offered.

"Good. We will need cloth. Can you find cloth and boil it in water, please?"

"Sure, I'll take care of it," said Gee. "I'll use a piece of shirt."

Doc, Lieutenant Lattimore, Captain Fitzsimmons, Colonel Black, and Colonel Williams were soon summoned to the guard room.

Yamada glared at them from behind his desk as they filed in. There were two other Japanese soldiers there who wore little shooting stars sewn to the rank insignia patches on the upper left sides of their jackets. Doc and Captain Fitzsimmons were so much taller they looked down upon Yamada. And obviously he didn't like it.

"Sit," he ordered, pointing at the bamboo floor. "Sit, sit, sit!"

They sat cross-legged on the bamboo poles.

Yamada strutted around to look down upon them. "Fred Quick, your American — I make example. Understand-kah?"

"He meant no harm," Fitzsimmons said. "Freddie Quick sang because he was scared and hungry. He meant no disrespect."

Yamada scowled. "Man speak while Japanese officer speak! *Joto nai!* No good!" He waited to make sure they understood. He sucked his gums then, as if to make a transition in thought. He motioned to one of the men with shooting stars. "My engineer is Lieutenant Mashita." Mashita bowed slightly to let them know who he was. "Mashita will tell you what to build and how much work to do each day. You must obey Mashita. My second in command is Sergeant Kosha." Kosha also bowed slightly. "Kosha will see that Mashita's orders are carried out."

They stared at him in stony silence.

"Understand-kah?" he asked.

They said nothing.

"You, Colonel Williams and Colonel Black, you are in charge of Australian prisoners. You, Captain Fitzsimmons, you are commander, Americans. Both of you will tell your men to obey all Japanese instantly, otherwise they will suffer consequences."

And still the men didn't blink an eye.

Eating could have been a cheerless affair, yet it soon became obvious that the Americans would not let it be that way. They found something to laugh about, even while waiting in line in the dark for dirty rice and watery soup. Henri understood less than half of what they said, but no one could mistake the continuous tittering, joking, and laughing.

The sailors and marines had mess gear and clothing shared by the soldiers, thus everyone had utensils of some kind. There were no lights; but then perhaps it was best not to see what we were eating. It was tasteless, but it filled the voids and temporarily stopped the hunger pangs.

We turned in early because there was nothing else to do, yet it was a long time before we settled down. This was the first time any of us had tried to sleep in a jungle. As night closed in with its eerie sounds we lay there listening, commenting on this sound or that, trying to guess what it was. A series of cackling sounds and a loud, blood-chilling scream made us freeze into silence. It sounded close.

A few seconds elapsed before the nervous conversation began:

"You hear that? Sounds like a woman in agony!"

"Betcha it's a hyena."

"That your cousin, Pinky? Th' gal you wus tellin' me about?"

"Which gal?"

"You know which gal."

"No, Bird Dog, it ain't her. Can't be. Her voice is a tad purtier'n that."

"Betcha it's a fuckin' hyena."

"Oh, yeah?"

"Shut up and listen."

"This is Frank Buck country, folks. Ah'll betcha it's a wildcat."

"No way, Caribou!"

"Betcha it's a fuckin' hyena."

"You wanta bet?"

"How much you got?"

Great peals of laughter spread its contagion until dozens of men were splitting their sides, drowning out the sounds from the jungle, and more.

Eventually there was enough silence to hear the scream again.

"Yep, ah reckon you're right. Folks, it *is* a hyena."

And there was more laughter.

Henri sat on his blanket, no doubt wondering what was so funny.

9

Doctor Without Credentials

"Surely there is order in the universe, some purpose in all this," Doc muttered half-aloud, standing in the chill before daybreak, no doubt hurting from hunger like the rest of us were. We were watching the swaying lanterns of the guards arriving for roll call. "It is in the nature of things that without despair there can be no hope, without darkness no daylight," Doc said. "There has to be meaning. Even if we can't see it."

As dawn approached we were eating rice and watery soup. And as sunlight burned through smoke from the kitchen, we were standing in a semicircle in front of a shack used for tool storage. The men were wearing worn shoes, some barefooted, all in bits and pieces of uniforms, some stripped to the waist. We each had a full canteen of water boiled in the kitchen cauldrons. And in our mess kits we carried a canteen cup of dirty rice and watery soup mixed together to be eaten at noon.

Four Japanese engineers stood off to one side of Lieutenant Mashita as he explained how we would work using the few words of English he knew, emphasized with sign language and grunts. The chain of command would be from him through the Japanese engineers down to the prisoners' officers who would act as foremen, and then to the workers, the peons. We would be "same-a same-a" as slaves. We would have no voice.

He held up a bamboo pole, a *"yo-ho"* pole, he called it, six feet long, two inches in diameter. Poles like this would be used to carry rice sacks filled with dirt.

He laid an empty sack on the ground to illustrate, winding a piece of bailing wire around the top left corner, looping it over and tying it around the top right corner. Another wire was similarly looped from the bottom left and right corners, then both loops were placed over the pole. Two men would carry dirt shoveled onto the sack. "So's-kah? So's-kah?" Mashita grinned, nodding his head. The two-man teams would have to carry the poles on the same shoulders, one man walking directly in back and in step with the other, he cautioned, otherwise their shoulders would be gouged and soon become painful.

"Kogya nai, kogya nai," he said, illustrating the wrong way; *"joto da, joto da,"* he said, showing the right way. "Okay-kah?" he asked. He grinned a lot. It was unbelievable that they expected to complete a railroad with *yo-ho* poles and shovels. "Like slaves of ancient Egypt," Tom McFarland muttered.

Mashita was short and fat and appeared to be good-natured enough. Sergeant Kosha was thick, short, and expressionless.

Twelve men were equipped with picks and shovels. Their job was to dig dirt from the tops of two hills, where trees and roots had been removed by an advance party of Burmese, and to load dirt on the sacks which the others would carry into the valley to build the roadbed between the two hills.

Yamada got the last words in. "You will work very hard," he said. "You will work quickly. Do not talk. Save energy for work. It is better if you enjoy your work."

"Crap," Bird Dog muttered. Apparently, the engineers didn't hear him.

"Isuduke! Isuduke!" Mashita yelled, waving his arms toward the gate.

"That means you are to follow him," Yamada said.

"Isoge! Isoge!" the guards shouted.

"Isoge means hurry. Speed-o, speed-o!" Yamada said.

We went out through the gate two abreast, officers up ahead with Hatashi and Mashita, Americans bringing up the rear, singing — marching in step with bare feet in the cool dirt, singing as if to taunt the Japanese, but actually to keep our own morale intact.

The line stretched single-file in a long loop between the valley and the hill, men going down the hill burdened with heavy sack-loads of dirt, those going up returning with empty sacks to be loaded. As the sun rose, the temperature climbed. It was hot, dusty, tiring, boring — endless.

We were allowed a ten-minute rest break at mid-morning, a thirty-minute stop for lunch, another ten-minute rest in mid-afternoon. We worked until almost dark. By the time we trudged into camp and lined up for the same kind of slop we had had that morning, it was dark and cold. No one was singing.

Doc got in line at the kitchen with the rest of us. I had accidentally scratched my right knee on a piece of bamboo, it was infected, and I wanted Doc to have a look at it, after we had eaten. So I stood right behind him when he got his ration, wondering aloud what kind of food his wife and children were being fed.

To help discourage mosquitoes and curious animals, we built bonfires between buildings. It was the only illumination. Doc sat near me on a log as he sipped the soup, forcing the tasteless rice down.

Colonel Black came down the aisle.

"Glad you're with us, Doctor Hakking," Black said. "Did the Japs give you any medical supplies?"

"Hekking, please. Not Hakking," Doc said. "I have only a few ampules of Neo-Salversan which I am not supposed to have. I took them from the Japanese in Timor."

"Is that all?"

"Yes, that's all."

Black paled. His jaw tensed. "No quinine? No iodine or first-aid medicine?"

"Nothing."

"Well, that's that," Black sighed, lifting his hat to scratch his head. "Have you come to know our Colonel Wiggins yet?"

"Yes. And no."

"Well, I presume you will be going back and forth to Than-byuzayat."

"That is Japanese decision. I have no idea."

"Yes. Well, I suggest you get to know Dr. Wiggins. He knows

tropical medicine. He'll be able to teach you a thing or two, I'll wager."

"Of course," Doc said. "Thank you."

I wondered why he had said nothing about his own training.

"What about medical equipment?" Black asked.

"I have only this stethescope."

Black looked grimly determined. "I'll speak to Yamada."

"Be careful," Doc warned. "I already spoke to him."

Black left. Doc sat silently for a few seconds. He called after Black. "By the way, is Captain Fitzsimmons here?"

"Yes. Do you know him?"

"I met him in Singapore. I thought perhaps —"

"I shall say hello for you," Black said.

"Ask him if he remembers me," Doc said.

"Of course. I shall."

Packrat McCone came by and stuck out his hand. "McCone," he said. "Packrat, they call me. You need anything — tin cans, bottles, thread, safety pins, old shoes — just ask ole Packrat."

"Yes. I heard about you from Slug Wright. Thank you." Doc sat back down with his mess kit.

Packrat was not ready to leave. "I also have some boards, a piece of canvas, some twine, a British canteen, and the makings of a first-class bomb."

"Bomb?"

"That's right. Some Jap cartridges I've hidden away. I can take out the powder and use some twine for a fuse. My problem is making a cap. Now, I figure I can use the bottom of a British canteen for the container. You partition it off —"

"You did say 'bomb'?" Henri said.

"Yeah. Boom! Pow! That kind of bomb. You know?"

"Gawd! Why do you want a bomb?"

"This is war, Doc. We use 'em to fight with, remember?"

"You mean to kill with."

"Yeah, that's the idea."

"I am not interested in bombs. I could use a suture."

"A suture?"

"It is like a needle."

"Oh, yeah. I know what you mean. If you need a suture, I'll make you one."

"Just like that?" Doc snapped his fingers. "I ask for suture, you make suture?"

Packrat snapped his fingers. "Just like that. No sweat, Doc."

I could tell from the way Doc acted that he only half-believed McCone. I finally got him to look at my knee. I had only scratched it, but already it was swollen. He didn't like the looks of it. "There is some infection," he said. "I should send you back to Thanbyuzayat where they may have some powdered iodine. Meanwhile, let's watch it closely for a day or two. Stay off of it as much as possible."

Black came back around that evening with Fitzsimmons. Fitzsimmons must have told him something about Doc, because Black was now much friendlier. The three of them had a lively, animated discussion that lasted late into the evening.

The next day the Japanese camp commander told Doc he was to go back to Thanbyuzayat in the supply truck. Those were orders. There was no argument. Doc told the Japanese major that I, too, should go to the Thanbyuzayat hospital. At that time, the routine of who was to go, and when, was not firmly established. So I was put on the truck with Doc.

Wiggins had requested that Doc be sent back. He had convinced Nagatomo that there had been a mistake: Doc was not supposed to have left Thanbyuzayat in the first place, but was to have received "training" in tropical diseases from the senior Australian and British doctors. Only after that was he to have received an assignment to one of the work camps.

Over the next few days, Doc seemed to pull himself into his own shell. He obviously respected the British and Australian doctors, and I knew he tried to work with them. But it was most distressing to him, discovering how different their approaches were to the treatment of tropical diseases. There were no medicines to carry forth the kinds of treatments they knew — treatments almost all doctors knew. Those years he had lived around tropical diseases in Java, absorbing his grandmother's teachings; the five years he had spent in Celebes, learning to improvise, treating the Towana and other natives for every tropical disease imaginable, often with herbs from his own garden — obviously he was light-years ahead of these doctors in practical experience, yet everything he did was supposed to be approved by them.

What he did not have was senior military rank, or any proof of what he knew. To the British and Australians — to any military group — rank was the thing, possibly the only thing, that implied the kind of knowledge or brains one was supposed to have. No rank, no brains. A captain was hardly a senior officer in Colonel Wiggins's eyes, particularly a forty-year-old doctor in wartime who had risen no further than that. And the fact he had no records and there was no other officer present from the Colonial Army to vouch for his level of expertise, these were negatives that cast grave suspicions, as far as Wiggins was concerned.

Doc had no records because the Japanese had confiscated those that were not burned when the hospital in Kolonodale was deliberately torched by the Dutch army. For him it would have been unthinkable to go around shouting to the world the nature of his medical accomplishments.

Doc told me that no matter what he said or how he said it, it would come out as self-serving and boastful. That was the reason he would say nothing.

Doc lapsed into long hours of silence, talking to no one. Not even to me.

When they bothered to ask, he told those around him he was not feeling well. He lay on the shelf, looking at the canvas painting of May, dozing, allowing himself to drift in and out of a state of semiconsciousness. He would not take a bath. He quit eating. There was nothing I could do to snap him out of it.

I went to another doctor, a young English captain, to get attention for my knee. All the English doctor did was bathe it in hot water and wrap it in clean, sterilized rags which were at least boiled in water.

I felt that no one knew who Doc really was, and that it was becoming increasingly obvious that no one cared. I told the British doctor about him, and I asked him if he would try to do something for Doc.

When I awoke that one morning and saw Doc lying in his own filth and stench, I think I realized that he had given up: he wanted to die. His mind had drifted back in time to a place on northeast Celebes, and he was mumbling something about Abdul.

"Whatever happened to Abdul?" I asked him.

He opened his eyes, briefly, then closed them again.

"Please tell me what happened to Abdul," I begged.

Doc could not resist telling a story, even when he was half-dead. In his own circuitous way he began, falteringly, at first, to tell me about his final days with Abdul.

On Celebes he had what amounted to his own private hospital in Kolonodale. It was supplied, staffed, paid for by the Dutch government, with no one to tell him how to run it. This I thought was rather curious, since he was only a young lieutenant supposedly being punished. Yes, he said, he thought that too, at the time. He said he had an endless supply of patients from as much of Celebes as he felt he was able to serve; no invoices to send out, no bills to pay, very little paperwork — a learning opportunity few people in the medical world would ever have.

Of course, equipment was extremely limited; staff consisted of uneducated Malaysians who would be trained only if he trained them, and he could rarely get the quantity of medical supplies he needed — thus forcing him to make do. But he had *oma*'s black book and his memory to serve him, and he supplemented the few medical supplies the army sent with an herb garden he grew behind the hospital, much like the one his grandmother had in Surabaya. He had his Zeiss microscope from his Leiden University days. For recreation, he had the villagers build a swimming pool near his house.

Because he loved the islands, and because he had made up his mind to make the best of his "punishment duty," what had been a nightmare for others condemned to serve on the Celebes was just the opposite for him. He smiled. "It was a learning experience of a lifetime."

His second child, Louise ("Loukie"), was born in Kolonodale in 1932. His family lived so much unto themselves that after Loukie was born the rest of the world seemed far removed. Letters and newspapers from The Netherlands talked of the deepening worldwide depression: of hunger, anger, and fear spreading across the face of Europe. But Europe was 10,000 miles away, news was three months old by the time it reached them, and it was difficult to react to it. Of course they were affected by the depression: supplies became even more limited than previously, because commerce between the outside world and the East Indies came to a virtual standstill. But economic times could not have been as bad for them here as they would have been in The Netherlands, Germany, Belgium, or in other parts of Europe. The Hekkings could not have felt the futility the Germans experienced, where money was so worthless an ordinary laborer carried home his weekly pay in a wheelbarrow.

Doc was told that year by his boss, Colonel de Vrieze, that he was being transferred to take over the army hospital in Surabaya. Another doctor would be arriving to take charge of the Kolonodale hospital, a Lt. Karel van Avnik, who would be there not on punishment duty but to handle the busy hospital that the one in Kolonodale had grown to be. Doc had no choice. He and his family would sail to Java, taking only their personal belongings.

It was customary to leave domestic help behind. Ordinarily, in a transfer like this, the routine would have been to sell off all of the larger pieces of furniture in a "vendutie," a festive kind of auction, where people came, visited, bought things, and had their servants carry the larger pieces away. In this case, there was no auction, as such. The other officers simply bought the larger pieces and paid a decent price, realizing that Doc and May would need the money to furnish a house in Surabaya.

They would also have to find new domestic help in Surabaya, since servants were never transferred unless they had been with the family for many years.

Doc and May were in the garden talking when Doc told her about the transfer. Abdul was in the stable within hearing distance. Doc saw him — there one instant, gone the next.

The day after Colonel de Vrieze and his party left, Doc called the domestic help together to tell them the news. It was not a pleasant thing to have to do. May was crying. So were some of the others. "Going away?" asked Takir, the gardener, tears gathering in his eyes. Most Indonesians who knew Doc called him Mister Doctor, or Pa, short for Bapak, or father, a term reserved for older persons or those they considered to be teachers.

Behind Takir was Baboe Tjoetji, the woman who did the laundry; Kookie, the female cook; and Koeda, the boy who looked after the horses. All were there, and Doc wanted to know what Abdul had been up to, mingling with the domestic help, talking to Takir.

No one said anything. They stood looking at the floor.

"There is a nomadic quality about Abdul," May observed. "As much as he loves you, one of these days he will leave Kolonodale."

"Did Abdul say anything about leaving Kolonodale?" Doc asked Takir.

Takir could not hide his feelings of guilt. It was this honest, open quality about Indonesians that endeared them most to Doc. "Last night," Takir said, "Abdul talked of going on a journey, a very long journey, by himself. He heard you talking. I was not to tell you."

"Did he say he heard what we talked about?"

"Yes."

"Then you already know why I've asked you here."

With pained looks on their eyes, they said nothing. Doc studied their faces. There was not a single one of them he wanted to leave behind. They were as much a part of him as if they were his own flesh and blood. They felt it, as much as he and May did: this was not a master-servant relationship. It never had been. Leaving one of them would be like leaving a brother or sister. It was painful to know he would have to leave every one of them.

He stood looking at them for a few moments, unable to speak. He turned and walked rapidly away.

Lt. Karel van Avnik and his wife, waiting for Doc and his family to leave, were staying in small, cramped, temporary quarters, anxious no doubt to move into the large house. But before he sailed, Doc was determined to make the rounds of the sick with the new doctor. He particularly wanted to visit the Towana one more time. Unlike other natives for miles around, the Towana would not leave the mountains and come into Kolonodale, no matter how sick they were. And he was particularly concerned about the health of a young Towana woman named Radan who had almost died in childbirth a week previously. She was small, and the child was unusually large. Radan's mother and father were dead. And the father of her child for some reason had apparently gone away before the child was born. Abdul was the only one who was with her at the time she almost died.

Doc said he and van Avnik rode horseback as far up the mountain as they could, then got off and led the horses, picking their way through underbrush and around trees until they were near the top where the Towana lived. The Towana had long since stopped hiding from Doc. One of the young men, Paku, guessed he had come to check on the young woman, and he led them directly to a newly constructed lean-to at the edge of the clearing. It was like the one he and Abdul had built on their first trip to the mountain together, only this one was larger and enclosed on all four sides.

"She and the baby are here?" he asked Paku.

Paku grinned. "Oh, yes!"

"Did her man build this shelter, Paku?"

Paku laughed. "Oh, yes!"

"Is her man in there?"

"See for yourself!"

Before Doc could look inside, an opening in the side of the lean-to moved, and through it emerged Abdul — grinning, holding the tiny infant.

"He is a healthy boy, Tuan! Look. Isn't he beautiful?"

"Yes, Abdul." He took the infant and almost from habit found himself checking its heart, lungs, and stomach. He handed it back. "It appears to be a winner. How is Radan?"

"Radan is also healthy. She is fine. She is very happy."

"Has the father returned?"

"Yes, Tuan. He has returned."

"Is he inside with her?"

They stood facing one another. And suddenly, Doc knew. Abdul was the father. Abdul knew the rule that he was never to touch a Towana woman. But Doc decided this was not a time to admonish him.

Doc said he felt great compassion for Abdul. "You know what this means," he said.

Abdul nodded. "Yes, I know what it means. Radan will never leave the mountain. She would die in village far away. She must stay here, and I will stay. From this day forward."

Doc said they stood looking at each other for some time. "How about her people? Will they accept you?"

"In time. They must," Abdul said.

Doc went in and inspected the girl, pleased to see how well the stitches had healed. He checked her heart, lungs, blood pressure, and temperature. She appeared to be normal, considering the ordeal and the length of time that had elapsed.

Doc stood in the opening of the lean-to, prepared to leave. "You are responsible now," he said to Abdul, nodding to the girl, motioning with a sweep of his arm to include the Towana people.

"Yes, Tuan. I am one of them. They are a part of me. We are one."

"I shall miss you, Abdul," Doc said. "Goodbye, my friend."

"And I shall miss you, Tuan. It will never be the same."

Abdul followed Doc to join van Avnik outside. He stood with tears in his eyes, holding the tiny infant, smiling, nodding as they mounted their horses.

Doc said he heard van Avnik turning his horse to follow him back down the mountain. He didn't look back. They rode in silence. He said it was as though the same omnipotent power that had brought Abdul and him together now had separate tasks in store.

"And that was the last time you saw him?" I asked.

"Yes. That was the last time."

Doc dropped off to sleep shortly after that. The young British captain, the doctor who had bandaged my knee, came by. He did a double-take. Apparently, he thought Dr. Hekking was dying. He stood over him, trying to get him to open his eyes.

"I say, old chap," he said. "Are you in there?"

10

The Grand Design

"What do you want?" Doc asked.

"You've been like this for three days," the British doctor said. "Come on, sit up. I'm not going to let you die here."

Doc glared up at him. "Go away."

"Not likely, old chap." The man had Doc by the shoulders. "This is no bloody hospital, you know. Sit up!"

Doc rose to a sitting position and saw the mess tin of food on the shelf nearby.

On top of dirty, steamed rice was a boiled egg — a real chicken egg. I don't know about Doc, but I might have considered killing someone for that egg.

"Where did you get that?" Doc asked.

"Why give a damn?" I exclaimed.

"You don't want it?" the Britisher asked.

Doc grabbed it.

"That's a good chap. Now eat it. Sorry, old bean, all I have is a spoon. Would you like me to peel it?"

Clutching the egg closer, Doc shook his head, obviously afraid to turn loose. He cracked it and began to peel it. I had never noticed the wonderful aroma of a boiled egg. My stomach ached from hunger as I watched.

"Fine," said the British captain, grinning. "Eat every bite of it. Eat the rice too. Get on with it now, I say."

Doc ate like a man half-starved, scooping rice to his mouth with the spoon.

The young captain also gave him a tin of hot tea. "Who is the lovely lady in the painting? Your wife?"

Doc nodded.

"Quite beautiful! Is she in Holland?"

"Timor. The Japanese have her," Doc said. "They also have my two children. The Nazis have my homeland. The Japs have my family and my beloved islands —"

"Your family will probably survive. But you won't, if you don't get off your bloody back!"

"You don't know that. You know nothing."

"I know you're alive, Dr. Hekking. I intend that you stay that way."

"Why?"

"You're a doctor, and we need all the bloody doctors we can get."

"How do you know I am a doctor?"

The British doctor nodded toward me. "Your friend told me." He grinned. "Also, I took the liberty of looking inside your bill-fold."

"You had no right to do that. But then, that is more than your Dr. Wiggins did. He never bothered to ask to see my wallet."

"Wiggins? That old toad? Ha!" the Englishman scoffed. "Don't fret about him. For now, fret about yourself. Then start to think about the others. They need your help."

"Who are you?"

"Dr. Anthony Quimby. Captain Quimby, actually. London. At your service." Quimby gave a ridiculous salute.

"Who sent you to me?"

Quimby laughed. "An angel, of course."

Quimby took the mess gear and turned to leave. He stopped. "Oh, by the by, there's a chap out here who wants to see you. A Yank. Won't talk to anybody else. If I let him in, will you talk to him?"

"No."

"Fine. I knew you would —"

"NO, I said!"

Quimby was gone. Perhaps he *was* an angel. I never saw him again. No one had ever heard of him. No one I asked, at least.

Moments later, Glen Self hobbled in and stood over Doc, staring down with black penetrating eyes set deep under heavy eyebrows. "You will help me, Doc, I know you will," he said. It was not a question. It was a statement, overflowing with hope.

Doc remembered him: the one with the bandaged leg he had seen on the field that first day in Thanbyuzayat. He raised his head enough to see the bandage, which was badly soiled.

He flopped over on his side. "I can do nothing," he said. "I have nothing. Go away."

Self stood there. "I heard you talking to Dr. Wiggins. I don't want to lose my leg, Doc. You gotta save it. Please!"

"You shouldn't be standing on it!" Doc said, rolling back over, raising himself up on an elbow. "Who are you?"

"Glen Self. Lubbock, Texas."

Doc reached for the bandage, his hand shaking. He must have suddenly realized what he was doing. He stopped and looked at his hand as if it belonged to someone else. He stared up into trusting eyes, into a pleading face.

"There is nothing I can do," he said, shaking his head. "I have no medicine and nothing to bandage it with. Can't you see? I am quite helpless." He lay back on the mat and rolled over with his back toward Self.

"You can help," said Glen. "If anybody in the world can save it, you can."

"Go away," Doc said.

Self shrugged. He looked down at his leg, then started to turn away. He stopped and turned back around. "I just know you can save this leg, Doc. All you gotta do is believe you can."

Glen Self must have touched a nerve. It was as though Doc had known this man for a long time: as if he had known that that Texan would be standing there, saying the exact words he was saying.

He rolled over to face Glen. "Why are you here?" he asked. "Think. You do not know me. You saw me one time only. You know nothing about doctors, nothing about me. You see I am a sick man! I have no shave in four days. Do I look like a doctor?"

"Yessiree, you shore do."

"Please! I have nothing! How can you say I look like a doctor?"

Self nodded his head, an expression of firm belief. He smiled, with tears gathering in his eyes. "I jist know you can save my leg."

"No one has ever shown so much confidence in me — not even my *oma*, or my mother or father, or sister, or brothers, or my wife May. Certainly none of my instructors!"

Self wiped his nose on his sleeve and kept grinning.

Slowly, Doc reached out and began to unwind the filthy bandage. When he looked up, Glen Self was nodding, tears glistening in his eyes.

The ulcer was as big as Doc's hand — one of the largest Doc said he had ever seen. It had eaten all the way to the bone, and the bone had turned black. Self had to be in terrible pain. The miracle was that he was able to stand, much less walk the hundred yards from the main hospital building to get to Dr. Hekking.

"How did you know where I was?" Doc asked.

"I didn't. Something brought me here. I am not sure what it was."

"It was an angel," I said, chuckling.

I could see the change in Doc's face, a change in his entire body as he looked at Self's leg. The man was coming alive. "This will have to be scraped very soon," he said.

"Do what you gotta do, Doc. I know you scrape these things. I can take it, so long as you don't cut it off. It can't hurt no more'n it already does."

"Oh, yes it can. And it will. It will hurt very much more. We have nothing to ease the pain, you see? That is the pity. Men will have to hold you. It is too bad we must do that. But if we are to hope —"

"Then there is hope, isn't there?"

Doc looked him square in the eyes. "Yes. A little."

Glen Self grinned. "As long as a man has a little to hope for, he can take jist about anything, don't you reckon?"

"Yes," Doc said. "As long as a man has something to hope for."

I believe that during those few seconds, a great change came over Dr. Henri Hekking. He must have realized it wasn't just medicine we needed. He knew he had something else to give us beyond medicine, and it was then that he made up his mind to give it. The opportunity was all around him, yet, temporarily, he had been so busy feeling sorry for himself that he had failed to realize it.

His grandmother's training, the reason for his being a doctor in the first place — these and many other thoughts had to have come into focus during those moments with Glen Self.

It was as though he had just decided that his entire life until then was part of a grand design, a preparation.

Part Two

11

A Ray of Hope

Doc struggled to his feet. "I cannot promise anything. I shall try," he told Glen. "Do not move about. Stay here. I may be gone for some time."

One could tell that he was lightheaded as he walked to the edge of the shack, staggering. He had let himself go for just three days, but because he was already on a starvation trend to begin with he would have a longer, tougher time regaining the strength he had lost. But he was obviously filled with purpose now, and there was no telling what he would try to do.

He said he felt he would have the concentration and energy to do what needed to be done, whatever that was.

I spotted a small bar of soap hidden under his shirt. He used it with water from his canteen to wash his face and hands, then dried them on his shirttail. After that, he looked as though he felt better.

The prisoners had barely started construction of the railroad, yet already the Japanese were hauling the most seriously ill back to this dreadful place, the Thanbyuzayat "hospital," dumping them like so many items of worn-out inventory. I was not considered a "worst case," and I was told by Quimby that I would soon be able to return to my outfit.

The British who appeared to run the hospital had allowed me to stay near Doc, but now that Doc was up and around, and because my knee was almost healed, they told me to stay around the so-called hospital. Made of bamboo, it stood at the center of the clearing, perhaps twenty by sixty feet in size, roofed with atap leaves like all other structures along the railroad. There was no water, no toilet facility, nothing inside except shelflike sleeping areas on each side of a dirt floor aisle. It was little more than a warehouse.

Bringing prisoners here was a way to get them away from "well" people. It was also a way to conserve food, since the moment patients arrived they went on half-rations — amounts below levels required to sustain life. Since there was little medicine, it was generally assumed that little could be done to salvage the men. So they lay like cordwood, emaciated, staring at the ceiling, most of them waiting to die. There were exceptions, like the soldier Glen Self. And there were other Americans, including Marine Sgt. Charles Pryor and Pvt. Marvin Robinson, who were also determined to make it. Doc vowed he would do his best to help them stay alive. Sgt. Dupler, unfortunately, was too far gone for anyone but God to help.

A makeshift operating table sat in an area partitioned off at one end of the building. Doc went there first to find fellow prisoners who would help him scrape Self's leg. Men who could stand to be near the operating table were the ones he asked first. If they could put up with the screams and smells of that, perhaps they could bear to help him, he suggested.

He asked a man with a scraggly beard, "Does it bother you, being this close?"

The man gave him a blank stare. "A little."

"I am a doctor. Will you help me operate?"

"Depends. An amputation?"

"No. I wish to avoid an amputation."

"Then I will do what I can."

"Have you helped before?"

"Once. With an amputation. Never that again."

The man's name was Rogers. Albert. Lance Corporal. From New South Wales. He had dysentery, but he said he felt he was up to helping as long as the idea was to try to save a leg. He would recruit three others.

Doc found Lt. Nicolaas Mast, a Dutchman who had lived in Japan for many years and who served as interpreter for Colonel Nagatomo. Mast spoke Japanese and English as well as Dutch. He agreed to escort Doc to Nagatomo. "He's quite approachable, really. His only interest is in finishing the railroad on schedule."

I didn't know what happened in Nagatomo's office until sometime later when Mast filled me in.

The Japanese colonel's tiny office was in the bamboo building used as headquarters. As he and Nicolaas stepped inside, Doc had the chance to see Nagatomo up close for the first time. He had short cropped hair, a round face, and puffed eyes. He looked to be about five feet seven in height. Perhaps forty, Doc's age.

The colonel motioned them to seats in front of his desk. He was watching every move Doc made.

"I am a medical doctor. I am also an herbalist," Doc announced, then waited for Nicolaas to interpret.

"Herbalist?" Nagatomo grunted.

"I know the plants that grow in the jungle," Doc said. "I know which are edible, which are not; which have medicinal value, which are poisonous."

Nagatomo was obviously interested. "He wants to know what you're driving at," Nicolaas said. "What is it you want of him?"

"I want to gather plants which may help men get well. He will send guards with me, of course. We will need empty rice sacks."

Nicolaas translated, then listened to several questions Nagatomo asked. "He wants to know the names of plants you look for," he said.

Doc reeled off the names of several. Nagatomo was as unfamiliar with herbs that grew in Burma as Doc was. He looked impressed, however. He said something to Nicolaas.

Nicolaas nodded his head. To Doc, he said, "The old boy is quite specific: he says if you try to use this as a method of escape you will be brought back here for execution. Beheading, actually."

"Please," said Doc. "I do not wish to play games. I have a sick man I am trying to help. When can we go?"

Again there was a brief consultation. "Right away," Nicolaas announced. "You will go right away."

Three guards accompanied Doc into the jungle. He explained later that the guards who carried empty rice sacks acted as though they were on some kind of lark until he started filling them. He found a broad-leafed weed that he recognized from field trips he had made with his *oma* in Java. He didn't remember the name of the weed. But he knew it was nonpoisonous, and that his grandmother had frequently used it for various ailments. When he and the guards came upon an abandoned village, the thing he looked for first were the stones upon which the Burmese ground the husks off rice. Knowing that the husks were rich in vitamin B, he scooped up enough of the dried husks to fill two sacks.

Glen Self sat on the operating table, stripped to the waist, sweating, legs dangling over the side, while Albert Rogers bathed the flesh around the ulcer with a cloth boiled at the kitchen and cooled in a section of bamboo. The others fought off the huge blue flies.

"I brought something from the jungle to stop your dysentery," Doc told Albert. "When we finish here I'll prepare it for you."

Albert grinned. "Thank you. All of us chaps has it. We all appreciate whatever you do."

"What kind of plants are they?" Glen asked, nodding toward the rice sacks on the floor.

"Oh, many different kinds. They do many marvelous things," Doc said. He was sharpening the edge of a tablespoon on sandstone, a rock the size of his fist. "Once we finish scraping that pus out we will make a cage for the open wound. Something to keep the flies out and to prevent you from bumping it, but something that will let the air in. You'll see."

I stood back as a silent observer. Glen looked around at the somber faces of the four men ready to hold him down. "You reckon you guys are up to this?"

They stared back without expression. "Ready when you are, mate," Albert said.

"How long is it gonna take, Doc?" Glen asked.

"I'll work as fast as I can. Two minutes. Three, perhaps."

Sweat stood on Glen's forehead. It trickled down through heavy, black, shaggy eyebrows. "Okay," he said. "Let's get it over with."

Doc rested his stethescope on several key spots across Glen's chest to listen one more time to his heart.

"What's my heart got to do with it?" Glen asked.

"Oh, very much. It is a strong heart. You are very strong man. You will come through this with no problem. You will be just fine."

Doc felt the edge of the spoon with his thumb to make sure it was sharp enough. He struck a wooden match the Japanese guard had given him, and he held the spoon to the blaze. He waited a few moments until the spoon cooled, then asked Glen to lie back, motioning at the same time for the four men to take hold of his legs and arms. He scraped lightly at first, removing the pus and loose surface material. He then told Albert to squeeze Glen's leg as hard as he could on both sides of the ulcer. Once the doctor started to probe deeper with the spoon, Glen let out a long, agonizing scream. Then, mercifully, he passed out.

Doc worked in silence, stripping away the rotted flesh, scraping the blackened bone. One of the men they called Gabe walked out of the shack to vomit.

Looking at the bone, Doc saw more than a tropical ulcer: a part of the bone had been chipped, and soon the infected part of that would have to be removed. He would need a surgical tool that resembled a chisel to take it out. And only one man he knew — the sergeant he called Butch from his staff in Tjamplong, who was in another prison camp — would know how to make it. If only he had the piece of metal and a way to shape and sharpen it . . .

Dr. Sagara came to watch, to write in a little notepad, to show his gold teeth when Doc looked at him. *"Joto!"* he said. "Very good work."

"I need a special tool," Doc said. "I have a friend who can make it . . ."

It took a long time to finish removing the pus. He scraped the bone, but none of this was a substitute for removing the piece of infected bone. That was still to come. He used strips of bamboo split with a pocketknife to make the open cagelike contraption to protect the open cavity. The four men used a stretcher made of bamboo poles and rice sacks to carry Glen, still unconscious, back to a shelf in the officers' quarters. He would be in pain and would run a temperature for several days. Doc wanted to be near him to offer as much encouragement as possible.

Doc lay totally exhausted following the operation. He was asleep when Dr. Wiggins awakened him. "You've done this quite on your own, haven't you," Wiggins said, scowling at the cage and at the cleaned sore. "I should have preferred that you consult me before you did this. I was going to amputate this leg. I may still have to do it to save this chap."

Sagara was there to look at the scraped bone. It appeared that he didn't understand what was being said. *"Joto,"* he grinned. "Very good work. Very good work."

"Why do you use that bird cage?" Wiggins asked. "For my patients I use a special poultice I make out of rice."

"There is problem with poultice in hot climates," Doc said. "Unless you have strong disinfectant and strong antibacterial medicine, the problem with a poultice is it provides a warm moist condition which is perfect as a breeding place for bacteria. Not so, when you make fresh air available. If you let fresh air get to the —"

"I know all about fresh air!" Wiggins interrupted. "I also know that bacteria is airborne."

"I will watch this very closely," Doc said. "More work needs to be done, but this man will recover, and he will not lose the leg, you will see."

"It will not be possible for you to watch this man. You have done quite enough already. You and your filthy rice husks! Oh, yes, I know all about that trip to the jungle. Your preparation for escape. Well, I don't want you to toy with the health of these men so you can plan your own escape! I am sending you to duty. You're quite ready to go, as far as I can see."

"I wish to stay for a few more days," Doc said.

"Joto, very good work," said Dr. Sagara.

Wiggins tried to ignore Sagara. "We already have two doctors here at base — three, if you count this slant-eyed devil. The Yanks at Kilo 40 need someone. Captain Fitzsimmons is asking for you. He's welcome to have you."

"Fine. Then I shall take this patient with me."

"No," said Wiggins. "I'm afraid not. He's in no condition to travel."

"One moment," Sagara interrupted. "I wish Dr. Hekking to remain here with his patient until we determine how successful his treatment is. I have spoken on that point to Colonel Nagatomo. Dr. Hekking will continue treating this patient for short time. The colonel is most interested in effectiveness of scraping method."

Wiggins was obviously dumbfounded. So was Doc, to hear such mastery of the English language coming from the Japanese doctor.

A red-faced Wiggins snorted a time or two, then left.

Later that afternoon Doc persuaded Albert to help him carry the two sacks of rice husks to the kitchen. This kitchen was like the one at Kilo 40: a roof of atap supported on four poles, a shield of bamboo and atap leaves lining the sides waist-high to keep rain from blowing in on whatever provisions they had. There were four large black cauldrons, one filled with plain water, one with a watery soup, and two with rice. Wood fires burned underneath. The soup was deceiving at this stage. The small amount of water buffalo meat floating around on top gave off a rich beef aroma, enough to intensify the hunger pangs. But by the time it was watered down to go around it would be almost tasteless.

"You want to do *what?*" the British cook demanded.

"Make cakes out of these rice husks," Doc said.

The Englishman grinned. "You mean you want me to put the same dirty stuff back in that we have worked so hard to get out?"

"Yes. If you please, thank you."

"Yer outta yer bleeding mind!"

Doc went through a long explanation of how the husks contained valuable life-sustaining vitamin B complex, "without which the men will surely die." He used every ounce of persuasion he could muster.

The Britisher finally raised his arms in a gesture of helplessness. "Okay. Assuming you're right, how do we do it?"

"Mix it in with cooked rice — here, I show you."

Doc mixed it in, kneading the mass into dough. He pulled out globs of dough to make several smaller balls. "Now, we drop these into boiling oil."

"Oil?" The cook laughed. "You don't say! Oil, the bloody blither says! There is no oil. What do you think this is, the Ritz?"

"Water, then."

"Dump it all in? Both bags?"

"All of it."

"I'm going to keep it apart from the rest, you can bloody well count on that."

"Fine," said Doc.

They made one cake for each prisoner. They were tasteless. But because they were different, and because Doc stood at the kitchen while they were serving them, making a fuss over each one and insisting it would be healthful, the men found themselves eating them, glancing around at one another as if they couldn't believe they were doing it.

Marine Corps Platoon Sergeant H. H. Dupler died. Sgt. Charles L. Pryor and Pvt. Marvin Robinson tried their best to help him. But the beatings he had endured in Batavia, plus dysentery on the ship en route, were too much.

Glen Self was convinced that Dr. Hekking had extraordinary powers. The soldier's leg was beginning to heal, and even though the infected part of the bone kept it from healing completely, he still had his leg.

Doc had described the instrument he needed to Lt. Sagara, and Sagara had made it possible for Butch to make it. The doctor would perform the bone operation as soon as he got the tool.

Glen Self and I were taken by truck to Kilo 40 the following day. Doc would soon follow.

My knee was also healing, and deep inside, through the change that had come over Hekking, I too was beginning to see a ray of hope.

12

The Food Quota

The supply truck from Thanbyuzayat arrived at Kilo 40, groaning in through the front gate, headlights stabbing across the open field into knots of prisoners gathering for roll call. The prisoners scattered out of the way as it creaked on by and came to a halt in front of the kitchen.

We had piled more wood on the bonfires and were stamping our feet in the chill, waiting for Yamada to come from his quarters.

Getting down off the truck was a tall, swarthy man with heavy dark eyebrows, a stethoscope dangling from his neck. He was dressed in the green uniform and leggings of a Dutch officer, an appearance disturbingly similar to that of the hated Nazis. I recognized him right away, and I was certain Captain Fitzsimmons and Lieutenant Lattimore did as well. But it was soon obvious that no one else did.

Doc and the two American officers came to stand directly in front of us near the center of the formation, while Colonel Black went back to the Australians.

We could hear Fitzsimmons asking Doc if he had any papers to prove his medical background, and we heard Doc say, "How is that possible? The Japanese took all my papers."

109

Bert "Bird Dog" Page stood on my right, eyeing the green uniform. I had known Bert from the *Houston.* He got his nickname because of his ears, and he had a way of noticing the little things about almost everyone, usually the nicer things. One day you realized you liked being around him and, while you may have wondered why, by then it didn't matter.

Bird Dog nudged me in the ribs. "Get a load of that! Looks like a damned Nazi!"

"That's Dr. Hekking. He was here before, remember?"

Otto Schwarz stood behind Page. "How do you know what a Nazi looks like, birdbrain?"

"You think they'd be crazy enough to put a Nazi in with us?" Marvin Robinson asked.

"I didn't say he *was* a Nazi, meatheads! I said he *looked* like a Nazi."

Captain Fitzsimmons interrupted. "Okay, listen up. Remember Dr. Hekking? I let him get away the last time he was with us. Well, we're fortunate to get him back, and we're not going to make that mistake again. I asked for him because when I talked to him in Singapore, I found out about his knowledge of the jungle. He knows tropical diseases, and how to treat them. I want you to cooperate. 'Hep' him as much as you can. You got that?"

"He got any medicine?" a marine, Tom McFarland, asked.

Fitzsimmons looked at Doc, and Doc shook his head.

"Nope, no medicine," Fitzsimmons said.

"If he has no medicine, and if he has no food, how is he supposed to hep?"

Doc leaned toward Fitzsimmons. "What is this word, 'hep'?"

"Never mind Tom. He's just kiddin'," Fitzsimmons said.

" 'Kiddin'? What is 'kiddin'?"

"Joshin'. Foolin'. Pullin' your leg. Get the drift?"

"Won't you please speak English?"

This ignited a burst of laughter.

"Quiet!" Fitzsimmons ordered. "I *am* speaking English." He looked at Doc's face and grinned. "Well, maybe a little Texan."

Doc looked at us and shook his head. "You are crazy people. I go back to Thanbyuzayat, please."

They laughed even louder. I was not a Texan, but it was great to hear them laugh.

"You should see what he did to Self's leg," Walter Grice said.

Grice was in Shanghai before the marines were pulled out, some sent to the *Houston* for "temporary" duty, thus he had the nickname "Shanghai."

Grice nudged Marvin Robinson. "You see Glen Self's leg?"

"Yeah. He unbandaged it last night. Worst lookin' thing I ever saw, still attached to a human body."

"The thing is, he's still got it," Grice said. "And it's gettin' better."

"Hey, Doc, I got you a suture!" Packrat McCone announced.

Doc obviously did not believe it, or know how to react. "That is very nice," he said, looking the other way.

McCone stepped through ranks to present the crude-looking needle, and Doc's eyes bugged.

"I made it out of a safety pin," McCone said, proudly. "Flattened one end with a coupla rocks. Gouged the hole with th' blade of a pocketknife. I also got you some twine you can use for thread. All you have to do is boil it to disinfect it. Think it'll work?"

"Of course it will work!"

"He's probably got a cannon somewhere too," someone said.

"I got the stuff to make one," Packrat grinned.

"And he ain't kiddin'!" Bird Dog said.

Doc held the needle toward the firelight. "Why, this is amazing! Superb! Thank you!"

"He's got the stuff for a what?"

"A cannon, knothead."

"If you need something else, just let me know," McCone grinned.

"Thank you, I shall. Packrat, you are genius!"

McCone laughed. "Yes, I know."

Guards were coming out of the guardhouse with lanterns, walking briskly toward us. It was still dark.

"Is Freddy Quick okay?" Doc asked. "Is he all right?"

"I'm here. I'm okay, Doc," Fred said. "Thanks for remembering me. Glad to have you back."

The two guards had notepads on clipboards. They were yelling *"Kodah, Kioutske! Tinko!"* ("Hey! Stand at attention! Count off!"). And things were getting back to normal.

But the count was stopped. Someone was missing.

While the Japanese guard waited, Fitzsimmons asked, "Anybody seen Jimmy Gee?"

"Yeah," said Quick. "We carried him out by the latrine. He's got the trots."

"It's worse'n that, Captain," someone back in the shadows said. "He's real sick. You better take a look."

"The flies will swarm those latrines at daybreak," Lattimore said. "It's no fit place. You guys take him back inside."

As the prisoners were lining up for rice and soup, Doc, Bird Dog, Marvin Robinson, Quick, and I were out by the latrines with Gee. We carried him back inside the American barracks, and Doc listened to his chest with his stethescope. Major Yamada was strolling not far away. He saw the commotion and came to see what was going on. We stood back out of the way.

"You fix?" Yamada asked.

Doc explained that he needed medicine. And when Yamada shook his head, telling him there was no medicine, Doc pointed at himself and then at the jungle. "I can find medicine in jungle. I am herbalist. You understand?"

This was too much for Yamada, who already viewed Doc as if he were a problem. "*Non-e-e-e-ee*, herbalist. You doctor."

Doc must have assumed Yamada could speak English better than he let on. "Yes, I am doctor. I am also herbalist. Herbalist doctor with jungle plants."

"Jungle plants?"

Doc nodded enthusiastically. "Yes, jungle plants. I know which ones are poisonous, which ones are good. Good plants help cure sick prisoners."

"You wish to go to jungle?"

"Yes. Right away, please."

"You go to escape, no?"

"No! Send guards with me. Provide rice sacks for herbs, and send guards. Yes, please?"

Yamada wrinkled his forehead. He started to leave. "Tomorrow, perhaps."

"Today! Now!" Doc insisted.

Yamada stopped and turned around, an impatient look in his eyes.

"This man die without medicine!" Doc explained. "Please!"

Yamada motioned for Doc to follow him. Minutes later, Doc and two guards were on their way to the jungle with empty rice sacks over their shoulders. We felt relieved, seeing that. Maybe Yamada had some compassion after all, we thought.

The jungle immediately around Kilo 40 was the same as the area surrounding Thanbyuzayat: plant life eaten over by wild animals and starving natives. But thanks to his grandmother's teachings, Doc was able to find a highly important weed: *cephaelis ipecacuanha,* a low-growing creeping plant with drooping flowers, its dried rhizome and roots excellent for the treatment of dysentery.

He brought back a sack full of the ipecacuanha roots. Yamada was at the gate to inspect the roots when he returned. Doc saw him watching from a distance as he boiled the roots, and he was aware of him standing in the entrance to the American barracks as he persuaded Gee to drink the boiled concoction.

By the next morning, Gee's condition had improved dramatically. He was surprised to see the Japanese commander taking an interest. Yamada came to the barracks early the next morning. Gee saw him coming and raised himself up on an elbow.

"You, okay-kah?" Yamada asked.

"I am better, thank you," Gee said.

It would be great to be able to say that Yamada took that much interest in the health of the prisoners. He may have, at first.

There were 194 men in Fitzsimmons's group, part of Group 3, or "Black's Force," the Australians called it. These were the first American prisoners sent to the railroad labor camps from Thanbyuzayat, and the first to be given so-called "command" assignments.

Lattimore and Doc were called into Yamada's quarters in the guardhouse and Lattimore was told he was to be prisoner mess-and-supply officer for Group 3. He was given a sheet of paper on which food allocations were spelled out in English.

"You will see that food brought into camp is prepared and distributed evenly among prisoners," Yamada told Lattimore.

Lattimore went over the paper with Doc and Captain Fitzsimmons.

The orders stated that each prisoner who worked was to have from 500 to 800 grams of rice per day. In reality, what he was getting was more like 250 to 350 grams, some rotten and unusable, all of a grade the natives usually fed to cattle. Each man was supposed to get 125 grams of meat per day, but that part of the order was a laugh. Prisoners were supposed to be fed 250 grams of vegetables per day. The vegetables were mostly melon — ninety-five percent water, five percent fiber — all of negligible food value.

All water was polluted by animals upstream. It had to be boiled. The weather was hot, the men perspired constantly, and because there were too few cauldrons in which to boil water, there was never enough to drink.

"What do you make of it?" Lattimore asked about the rations list. "Shall I go back in and let him know we know how far off the mark they are?"

"I don't see any other choice," said Fitzsimmons. "I suppose when this was written, they must have honestly thought these kinds of rations would be readily available. Anyway, you might approach Yamada with that attitude."

The guardhouse was actually a room at one end of a barracks in which the guards slept. Inside the room were three chairs and a desk. Usually, a sergeant sat at the desk. At the moment, Yamada sat there as Lattimore stood in the doorway. "You have question?" he asked.

"Yes, sir, I do," Lattimore said.

Yamada waved toward the chair. "Come. Sit."

He kept his silence as Lattimore went over the list, item by item.

When Lattimore stopped talking, Yamada asked, "Are you finish?"

"Yes, Major. I want you to know that we strongly object to this."

"We have no more food," Yamada said. "When we get more, prisoners get more. Be thankful for what you have. Be grateful you live. Okay-kah?"

"I am grateful to be alive. But our men cannot stay alive unless you improve the food situation. You and your guards and engineers are eating comparatively well, taking for yourselves the best of whatever is available. That water buffalo we had the other day — when it was butchered, your men cut off the best parts and ate the equivalent of steaks and boiled beef while the prisoners were lucky to get small bites of tripe and intestine and pieces of meat the size of teaspoons!"

"You are prisoners! You do not talk about the food the Japanese eat! Japanese are your masters! You are nothing but slaves, do you understand?"

Lattimore pulled himself up to his full height, about as high as Yamada's armpits. "You don't expect me to believe that, do you?"

Yamada growled down at him. "You are a slave!"

Lattimore waved the piece of paper. "Why do you make this list? Have you no intention of honoring it?"

Yamada's eyes bulged. He turned his back. "The list is what we hope to do — not what we can do," he said.

"You don't worry about a day of reckoning, because you think you'll win the war. Is that it?" Lattimore asked. "There's a day comin', buster. You'll see." He turned and walked out.

While Fitzsimmons was permitted to stay in camp most of the time — at one point he devised and carried out a desperate scheme to obtain medicine under false pretenses from nearby villagers — Lattimore was out with the men constantly, sharing whatever fate that came their way. Having been in enlisted ranks for several years, he was more attuned to their way of thinking.

Lattimore's father was a doctor, so he may have understood better than anyone what Hekking was trying to do. The modest, shy man spoke with a soft voice. He was short and frail-looking, and possibly because he was always trying to be helpful, he was liked by everyone.

A few evenings later, I saw Doc racing barefooted across the grounds toward the back of the kitchen. Realizing something was different, I followed him. The Japanese had killed another water buffalo and had helped the prisoners hang it up on a tree to be butchered. Again they had taken the best parts, and had caught its blood in a tub.

Doc saw that the prisoners were about to dump the blood on the ground a short distance back from the kitchen, and he raced to stop them. Before anyone could stop him, he grabbed the tub and emptied the contents into one of the kitchen cauldrons.

"That's a rice cauldron you're puttin' that in!" an Australian yelled.

Doc ignored him.

"Why are you doing that?" I asked.

He was poking wood beneath the kettle, stoking the fire. He didn't look up. "It is protein. Our bodies starve for protein."

"But, you expect us to eat that?"

"Of course. You will eat what you must to live. In Java, cooked blood is a delicacy."

"Java is a mighty strange country," I said.

I watched, ready to vomit, as the blood boiled and turned black.

Finally, as Doc stirred it around with a pole, it hardened and became grainy. He dipped some of it out with a spoon, blew on it to cool it, then tasted it, smacking his lips. A pleased look appeared on his face. "M-m-m-m-m-m," he said. "Very good! Here. You try it."

Other prisoners were gathering around, some more repulsed than others. The cooked blood was tough enough to chew. If it was good for us, and I had no reason to doubt that it was, I was determined to chew it and inject it. It tasted a bit like burned rubber with only a bare hint of beef liver. "Not bad," I lied, smacking my lips, trying to hold a straight face. "Excellent," I said, swallowing it.

Doc's face beamed. "See? I tell you so!"

Bird Dog's eyes were like saucers. "You're kiddin'! Gimme that spoon!"

Yamada came to roll call two weeks later to find that fifteen Americans and twenty Australians had diarrhea so badly they were unable to go out to work.

"Jungle medicine no work?" he asked Doc.

"Without proper food, no medicine work," Doc said.

Yamada winced. His eyes blazed as he strutted back and forth in front of our ranks, hands folded behind his back. Finally, he told Doc to stay in camp and he motioned for the guards to take the rest of us on out to work.

That day, Doc and two guards doubled the amount of ipecacuanha roots they brought back from the jungle. Additionally, Doc brought in a batch of tannin bark, the tea made from which would constrict the bowels and help in the treatment of diarrhea, he said. He also found a *kumiz kucing* plant — cat's mustache, he called it, using the Indonesian term (*folia orshosiphorns*, in Latin). It would help those with urinary infections.

Doc asked for separate vats, and he selected a separate location away from the kitchen. Yamada had the guards supply a container that held about five gallons of water. Bob Hanley and Slug Wright set it up and built a fire under it.

The doctor concocted one brew of ipecacuanha, like the one he had boiled for Jimmy Gee (who by now was recuperating); a second brew with *kumiz kucing;* and a third one with leaves that remained a mystery. It had a vile look about it, and a taste so putrid only the strongest (or sickest) could get it down. He wouldn't talk about its contents, except to say, "it's *good* for you." Some of us thought it was a kind of placebo, although we never voiced that thought to one another. We were barely twenty years old, and Doc told us we still had good immune systems. Thus, with luck, he said, we could survive most ordinary sickness. All we had to do was believe we could, Doc told us. The critical test would come when rainy season started.

We were beginning to trust him. At least, we wanted to trust him.

13

Breach of Protocol

After work, day after day, we lined up for Doc's foul-tasting brews, often cursing as we took a spoonful of this or a ladle of that. Always, with every dose he dispensed, we would hear his deep, reassuring "Take this, it is *good* for you," intoned as if each were a special communion.

One day I asked Noel Mason, one of the soldiers, "What do you think? Is this stuff any good? Or is he feeding us a line of horseshit?"

Mason was all teeth when he grinned. "Mostly horseshit. But if it works, what's the difference?"

In less than thirty days, however, diseases were increasing in types and severity despite Doc's medicine. I suppose we knew we were living on borrowed time. We were constantly hungry, and common sense told us that the longer we went this way the more susceptible we were to the many different kinds of tropical diseases. Yet it was not a subject to dwell upon. Instead, going back and forth to work, spending the long hours together on the *yo-ho* poles, we shared the best and worst parts of our pasts, and we dreamed together about the future. We rarely talked about the now.

Again Doc and Lattimore went to Yamada. "The men will die without better nutrition," Doc stated.

"The men have plenty food. I see." Yamada grinned, patting his stomach. "They are big with food."

"They are big with water," Doc said. "They are bloated, some with beriberi. The diet is not properly balanced."

"Balanced? *Non-ee*, 'balanced'?"

"Non-ee" meant "what do you mean?" but there was no one who could translate to Yamada what a balanced diet meant. The more Doc tried, the more confused Yamada became, or appeared to become. The Americans were not the only ones complaining bitterly. The Australians, British, and Dutch also badgered Yamada constantly. And eventually his responses became less civil.

Beriberi and pellagra resulted from inadequate nutrition, mainly the lack of vitamin B complexes.

We were struck right away with several different kinds of fever, all malaria-related, some more violent than others. One of the worst, we labeled it "monkey fever" although that was not the real name, was presaged by the arrival of a dozen large monkeys, possibly apes. They converged at the edge of the clearing one morning and stayed for four or five days, alternately friendly and scolding toward us, until a guard tried to kill one with a rifle. They fled screaming at that point, and a prisoner came down with the fever the next day. Whatever form of malaria it was, it caused an unusually high fever (there were no thermometers to tell just how high), hallucinations, and death in less than four days.

Glen Self's leg was slowly improving, but because of the ulcer's enormous size, it would take many months at best to heal entirely — if it ever did. Tropical ulcers of all kinds were greatly feared. Any kind of scratch on arms or legs, no matter how small, inevitably started an ulcer. The circular ulcers burrowed straight to the bone, widened in circumference, then filled with pus as skin tissue became involved. They started out small, and if they weren't treated — scraping, with no painkiller, was the only remedy we had — they could potentially be as bad as the one on Self's leg.

Amoebic dysentery *(endamoeba histolytica)* remained the most dangerous of all the tropical diseases. Its symptoms were severe pains in the large intestine, a constant desire to evacuate the bowels, and the discharge of mucus and blood. Without a way to heal the inflammation and curb the discharge, death followed in a matter of ten days to two weeks. Practically everyone in camp suffered from it sooner or later.

Without Doc's ipecacuanha and tannin tea, there is little doubt that everyone in camp could have died in less than three months. It struck indiscriminately, the strong as in the case of James Gee, as well as the weak. Gee had been among the first to contract it, and he was so far gone by the time Doc administered the ipecacuanha he had had the smell of death about him, the main reason the men had carried him out by the latrines.

Robert Hanley, a navy corpsman off the *Houston*, was Doc's first American medical aide. He helped sterilize needles and bandages, make poultices, administer whatever "medicines" there were — real or concocted — and do whatever else could be done to help the men. Soon, there were too many sick for two men to handle. Slug Wright, because he was often in camp ill, began to fill in where Hanley left off. Eventually, both men were helping Doc. The largest men available — Dave Hiner, James Gee, Tom McFarland, and John Owen, for example — were called in when teeth had to be pulled or ulcers reamed. Their job was to hold the patient down while Doc did what had to be done.

The roadbed at Kilo 40 was a grayish, swollen dragon lying between two hills: bloated with the odor of rotted jungle, fed by the long, continuous lines of two-man teams with *yo-ho* poles bringing dirt like putrid food from the tops of the two hills, dumping it into the many ravenous mouths.

The mound was almost finished the night Captain Fitzsimmons was told the men would be moving to another camp. He had often watched Hekking, Hanley, and Wright working together. A meticulous man himself — his hobby before the war was rebuilding and repairing firearms — he enjoyed watching others work with their hands. These three were particularly inventive, making splints out of split bamboo for broken bones, cagelike contraptions for open sores, poultices and medicines out of what looked like ordinary weeds. Each seemed to know what the other was thinking or planning to do next.

On November 28, 1942, three weeks following Doc's arrival, Fitzsimmons stood back, watching until the last man in the sick line went in and out of the "medical center," the tiny shack near the American barracks.

"You are doing well," he told Doc. "How do you like these crazy Americans by now?"

Doc laughed. "Well, I tell you. They never been anywhere or see the world until they come this time overseas. Some have never gone from home before. They are like young children made to act like men too soon. They have never read anything. They speak terrible English, like me. But you see, I think they are beginning to trust the old jungle quack. So I, of course, I like that very much."

"Why are you working so hard to help us, Doc?"

"I am a doctor. It is my job."

"I know. But it's more than that with you, isn't it?"

"Oh?"

"I've been watching you. You sleep very little. You're at it all day long, never stopping to rest. What is it, Doc?"

"I already tell you. It is my job."

"Okay. If that's the way you want it. The men like you. They think of you as their father," Fitzsimmons said. "Perhaps that's enough."

"Well, yes. Maybe."

"They think the good Lord may have put you here."

"Yes?" Doc beamed. "You see, that proves how crazy they are! But they are young. They will grow out of it."

"By the way, Doc. You never did tell me about that punishment duty you had in Celebes."

"You still remember that?"

"Sure. I've been curious ever since Singapore."

"Well, it was a little thing. Actually, it was not the fault of the Colonial Army so much, but the fault of two of my senior officers. They were at war with each other, quarreling, you know? And I got in the middle. My military troubles came, or rather they crept up on me, when I least expected them." Dr. Hekking led into his story.

He and May had started their honeymoon in early November of 1929 by visiting May's Aunt Corrie and Uncle Theodore Gielings in France. Attracted by the glitter of Paris, Uncle Theodore had run away from Holland at age sixteen, had lived in the city for several years, had learned to speak French fluently, and was able to show them around as only a native could.

After a week in Paris the Hekkings boarded a Dutch

ship in Marseilles bound for Indonesia. It had sailed from Rotterdam harbor November 14 with twenty-four other Dutch army officers and their wives aboard, plus a cargo of heavy plant machinery, wine, spirits, and special foodstuffs. The ship offered luxurious accommodations. Passengers were expected to dress formally for dinners, but there was little effort made to follow the rules of protocol normally adhered to by officers ashore.

Henri and May were often in the company of senior officers and their wives, chatting, laughing, oblivious to rank that was supposed to separate them. Because they were young newlyweds, they were included in all of the social functions; yet they were rarely in a situation where Henri had to pay for rounds of drinks or snacks. So the cruise served as a long, joyous continuation of their honeymoon — one that not even the wealthier people of the world could possibly have arranged.

They sailed east from Marseilles to Port Said, and on across the length of the Mediterranean past the coasts of Italy and Greece, the Middle East on their left, North Africa on their right. They sailed across the Red Sea to the Gulf of Aden, then eastward to Singapore and finally to Batavia, Java, completing the 9,900-mile voyage in four weeks. By the time they disembarked in Java, Henri said he was convinced that officers and gentlemen of the Dutch Colonial Army were among the finest on the face of the earth.

They arrived early in December. The army moved them immediately to a small, unfurnished house near the Batavia Army Hospital. Doc reported to Col. James de Vrieze, senior administrative medical officer, a tall thin man in his mid-fifties, devoutly interested in health care, not in the superficialities of army politics.

During a six-month internship Doc was expected to spend his time learning state-of-the-art methods of diagnosing and treating tropical diseases. The hospital was the largest in the Dutch East Indies, with the finest equipment available, ample medical supplies, and an endless supply of patients. He had learned the hard way at Leiden University not to advocate herbs his Grandmother Vogel had used. To the contrary, he had found life easier when he didn't mention them. To most doctors, those who used herbs to treat people — *"doekoens,"* they were called in Java — were only a notch above the early patent medicine men in the United States.

As an intern, Doc said, he soon became popular with the doctors because he made it a point to listen and to learn from them. He was popular with the nurses, too, as well as with other interns and the patients because he made it a point to find humor in as many situations as possible. Of course, he also tried to be helpful, and he avoided being a show-off. He and May became frequent party-goers, popular at officers' club dances as well as parties at houses on "officers' row."

The months raced by. Colonel de Vrieze promised Doc an assignment on the general hospital staff in Batavia. He would combine medical research with teaching. It was as if happiness knew no bounds, Doc said, "as if any apprehensions we might have had about a future in the army were groundless."

Then, a week before he finished internship, most men of the garrison, including doctors and interns, were ordered out on maneuvers. At the conclusion it was announced that the governor of the area, Willem van Zwaag, would be coming to visit the Batavia army base.

The base commander, Col. Jacob van Hoff, invited the new arrivals from Holland, including medical officers and officers of the regular army, to be there to honor the governor at a formal affair at the officers' club.

"I had vague misgivings about going," Doc recalled. "I had had minimal training in the protocol of such affairs. But then I remembered the cordiality that existed aboard that ship out of Marseilles, you see?"

When he was introduced to Governor Willem van Zwaag as he went through the reception line at the club, van Zwaag said, "I knew your grandfather, Freemason Hekking, who saved the lives of many people in Surabaya from cholera." Doc said he was profoundly impressed. If the governor had singled him out and was that friendly, who cared about protocol? The governor then told him he would like to chat with him later on as the party pro-gressed. Of course, Doc had no idea that such a courtesy extended by the governor had all the makings of a land mine.

He was seated with Lt. Jan van Lannen and two other officers he had met on the ship when Col. Jacob van Hoff's adjutant came to the table, introducing himself as Gover-nor van Zwaag's "errand boy" for the evening.

"The governor would like to talk to you now," he told Doc. "I believe he knew your grandfather." He pointed. "He's right over there, waiting."

Doc said he got up from the table immediately. "Ex-cuse me, gentlemen," he said. "Duty calls."

"Beware," said Jan van Lannen. "Remember the rules, Henri."

"What rules?"

"If you haven't learned them by now, it's too late."

Doc presented himself to the governor, who immedi-ately asked how he and his wife were enjoying Batavia. When he told him how happy they both were, the governor said he looked forward to meeting May on one of his future trips.

Doc was introduced to others at the table — a Major van Swieten, a Colonel de Haas, among others. He thought they looked at him strangely when, at the governor's urg-ing, he sat down to talk about his Grandfather Hekking.

It occurred to him that the senior officers looked some-what embarrassed. But that was their problem, not his, he thought at the time.

He was aware that he was doing most of the talking. But Governor van Zwaag seemed genuinely interested in Captain Hekking, master of a fleet of merchant ships, Hen-ri's grandfather — so what else could he have done but con-tinue? They were all interested in what he had to say — even Colonel van Hoff.

What was wrong, trading jokes with the governor? That's what the other officers were doing, Doc thought. He was not intoxicated: the fact was, he was a model of good behavior.

He got a hint of trouble when at last he returned to his table.

"You were out of line, sitting at that table," van Lannen told him.

"You're kidding! I was asked to sit there by the governor himself! What should I have done? Refused the governor of the islands?"

"Yes! By all means you should have declined! Politely, but without hesitation. By doing what the governor asked, you embarrassed the senior officers and yourself as well."

"I can't believe you are saying this! Are you sure?"

"Positively."

How could he have declined the governor's request without offending him? Doc wondered.

He remembered van Lannen smiling. "Don't be so worried," he said. "The offense is not all that serious. Really. They usually overlook things like this, particularly with new medical officers."

Doc said he did not realize how deeply in trouble he was until the following Monday morning. Colonel de Vrieze had sent for him.

"You stupid man, what have you done?" de Vrieze shouted. "Ignoring the most basic of rules. And now I have to send you, my prized pupil, to apologize!"

"Apologize — to whom?"

"To Colonel van Hoff."

"For what?"

"For making a mockery of protocol!"

"But the governor asked for me —"

"Go, Henri — this instant — before I put you in irons!"

Doc said it was a mile from the hospital to the administration building, regimental headquarters of the Colonial Army. He explained to the colonel that he had no car. Colonel de Vrieze picked up the telephone and ordered his chauffeur to bring his staff car around immediately.

"Take this lieutenant directly to Colonel van Hoff!" he yelled into the phone, then slammed it down. "Get out!" he roared, jabbing a finger toward the door. "Out before I throw you out!"

The driver said nothing as Doc got into the car. They were in front of the army base before he spoke. "Sir, are you going in like that?"

"Like what?"

"You're out of uniform, Lieutenant."

Doc said he looked down at himself. He had his pants, shirt, jacket, and hat on. His pants were buttoned. What other foolish thing did he have to worry about?

As he approached the administration building, enlisted men saluted. There was no hint that anything was awry. He told the sergeant of the guard that he had orders to meet Colonel van Hoff, and the sergeant announced him to the colonel and showed him in.

Van Hoff's gaze fixed on Henri's hands. His jaw dropped. "My gawd, you're unclothed! Where are your gloves? Your saber?"

"I was in a hurry —"

"How dare you! Coming here like that! Why?"

Doc grinned. "I am not sure. A half hour ago I was treating patients, doing something useful. I was told to rush over here to apologize — why, or for what, I am not quite certain —"

"Lieutenant, you're on report!" van Hoff bellowed.

Being on report was serious business in the Dutch army, Doc said. A black mark was put on the offender's record which, once entered, was there forever. It limited the rank an officer could hold, thereby denying him of housing and other amenities only those at the very top could enjoy. It even limited the amount of pension he could draw in retirement.

Doc said it meant nothing to Colonel van Hoff that Doc was rated as one of the top interns at Batavia hospital. Van Hoff never talked to doctors and nurses who evaluated interns. And besides, what a grand opportunity this was for van Hoff to embarrass his old enemy de Vrieze by making one of his prized interns look bad. He cited Doc for conduct unbecoming to an officer: sitting at the very same table with the governor himself, telling jokes, of all things. There were several witnesses to Dr. Hekking's behavior. Never mind why he had sat at that table. There could be no acceptable reason. Ignorance of the rules was no excuse; breaking them because of ignorance was probably worse than having knowledge of them and breaking them for some misguided purpose.

Doc was told he would be on probation for the remainder of his training period. Afterwards, for all practical purposes, he would be banished from the large garrisons and the obvious benefits on Java, and stationed in some remote, out of the way place, until he learned how to properly conduct himself.

Doc said his romantic attitude toward the army came to an abrupt halt.

The army's position was that in officers' training everyone without exception had an obligation to read the officers' manual and to know the rules. Of course, van Lannen was right: ordinarily, Doc would not have been punished at all. Young medical officers might be reprimanded, but they were rarely treated that severely for minor infractions of the rules. What Henri did not know was that the feud between Colonel de Vrieze and Colonel van Hoff was at fever pitch, and that he was in the direct pathway between them.

Fitzsimmons let the story sink in for a few moments. "If it will make you feel any better, you should know that American armed services are just as strict as yours when it comes to protocol. But it doesn't sound like protocol was the problem as much as the feud between two colonels."

Doc nodded his head. "That's exactly right."

"So your punishment was that tour of duty on the Celebes. Well, because of your punishment, we've got ourselves a better doctor. Tell me. Whatever happened to Lieutenant Nouwen and his wife, the two who were with you and May in Kolonodale?"

"I never found out. They were supposed to be in Surabaya. But when I was ordered there to take over the army hospital, they were gone."

"I'll bet May was happy to get back to a larger city."

"Yes. Very much so. And even though it was very hard work for me in Surabaya, I was pleased by then to have a different set of problems. That hospital there is the second largest in the East Indies. Before, the man who served as administrator had many assistants. I had one, only one. But we earned many commendations, that one assistant and I. He was good at paperwork, you know? That freed me up to be a doctor, which I liked very much, and we worked together as a team."

"You and these boys work well together as a team," Fitzsimmons noted.

"Yes. Both Hanley and Slug are excellent! They would be good anywhere."

Fitzsimmons waited around for a few minutes, then told Doc what he had really come to tell him. "Doc, Yamada tells me we're moving to Kilo 25 tomorrow. To the camp near Kun Knit Kway. What if you could stay here for the next batch of prisoners who come along? Would you want to stay?"

"Yamada gives me such a choice?"

"What if he did?"

"You do not pull my leg? You do not kid me?"

"I see you're learning Texan."

"Yes. Well, if I have such a choice, I tell you — I think I go with you guys. Okay?"

Fitzsimmons grinned. "You bet it's okay."

14

The Red Caboose

Shortly after the move back north to Kilo 25 it became evident that we were losing in the fight against starvation and sickness, despite Doc's medicines and best efforts. We had to have more food.

"We know the Japanese have eggs and *shindega,* the unrefined sugar. We know they're getting it in Kun Knit Kway," Lattimore said. "Some of our men have already been to the village. They traded for some of the stuff."

"Is that what I see wrapped in atap leaves?" asked Colonel Black.

"That's it," Lattimore said. "It's about the size and color of bricks. How much of it have you seen?"

"Actually not much. Two, maybe three loaves."

"Our guys, or yours?"

"Our chaps. I say, don't worry about it. They're careful around the Nips. They don't try to hide things like that from me, you know."

"Okay. Good," Lattimore said. "The question is, how do we get sufficient quantities to make a difference?"

"Perhaps we have to begin by asking what it is the Japanese want most from us," Doc said. "It is more work, yes?"

"Yes, and faster work. Yamada complains every day," Fitzsimmons said.

"The Japs should pay us," Lattimore said.

Fitzsimmons laughed. "Sure. Of course they should."

"I'm not joking. They should pay us."

"You've got to be kidding!" Fitzsimmons said. "They'll never do it!"

"Let's give it a bloody try," said Colonel Black. "What have we got to lose?"

It sounded like a ludicrous idea, at first. But Yamada had gone along with the jungle herbs, proving he wasn't entirely inflexible.

Doc, the two American officers, and Colonel Black went to Yamada with the idea. By now they had expanded on it and had convinced themselves it was pure logic: Yamada would get more work from his prisoners if he paid them at least a few pennies a week for eggs, raw sugar, and cigarettes, and if he gave them one day off a week. Surely such supplies in small quantities would be available at a nearby village, they suggested, without revealing that they knew the name of the village and the status of its wares.

What they did not know was that a similar suggestion had already come from headquarters and Yamada had elected to ignore it.

Yamada gave the appearance of walking around the idea for several days, mulling it over. Eventually, he said he would try it. He allowed one day off out of every ten, and he saw to it that prisoners were paid a few pennies each per week.

Once every ten days the guards brought small quantities of eggs, *shindega*, cigarettes, and cooking oil back from Kun Knit Kway. No one gained any weight as a result of it, but it boosted morale. And it may have contributed more to our health than we realized. At least it was a victory of sorts for the officers. "Chalk one up for our side," someone remarked.

We were not allowed to talk to natives who occasionally dared to approach the fence with food or cigarettes for barter. We were warned that talking or trading with them meant certain death by firing squad, or beheading (we might have a choice). But we paid little attention to the order. There were only a few instances we knew about where men were actually executed for trading with natives. At one time or another most of us, usually alone, went across the fence. Some, like Packrat McCone, John Owen, Marvin Robinson, and Eddie Fung, went more frequently than all the others combined. Fung, a Chinese-American, was bolder and more successful than most. His method on our days off was to slip into the village with items of clothing (usually from prisoners who had died), trade with the natives for food, hide the food in the brush near camp, then after roll call and late at night slip back out through the fence to bring the booty in.

Fung shared unselfishly with others, claiming he had a distinct advantage because "I look just like them."

I had had dysentery. I was physically weakened by it, and after work I could hardly wait to lie down.

"Look, I know you have that chess set," Gee said one evening. "You want me to teach you how to play?"

I lay on my part of the bamboo shelf, exhausted. "I don't feel like it," I said.

I hoped he would go away.

The work in Kilo 25 was laying crossties and rails, and the hours were the same: from first light until too dark to see after sundown. Working in the dark with rails and crossties was hazardous. One soldier, Walter K. Guzzy, had dropped a crosstie on his toe, and without painkiller Doc had had to remove the smashed toenail a piece at a time, using a pair of pliers. The men held him, and someone squeezed the foot to help deaden the pain. But his screams could be heard for a mile.

The bonfires at night discouraged tigers, leopards, snakes, and scorpions from coming in; they also provided warmth physically and psychologically. We were allowed to sit around them until approximately 9:00 P.M. On most nights, however, I was too tired, sick, and cold to stay up, and too depressed to want to talk.

An elderly Dutchman in the Batavia prison had given me the chess set. I had told him I didn't know how to play, but he had insisted I take it anyway. "Learn," he had suggested, tapping himself on the head. "Important you learn."

I had kept the set among my few belongings: the oil-soaked underclothes and a marine shirt, sleeves and shirttails torn off for bandages; shoes and a pair of pants donated by the army. The Japanese had taken my billfold. My only extraneous possession was the chess set.

"There's enough light to see by. Come on. I'll teach you."

"I'm too tired. I hurt all over. Forget it."

"Look, Charlie. Your mind is like the muscle in your arm. Either you use it or it gets flabby and useless. Come on. Get up off your butt."

The chess pieces were inside one of my shoes, wrapped in a piece of canvas painted like a chessboard. I pulled the set out and handed it over. "Get somebody else."

"It's you or nobody."

"Come on!"

"I'm trying to help you."

"Why?"

Gee tossed the set at my feet. "Damned if I know! Lay there and rot, for all I care!"

I scratched the lice in my eyebrows. "I lie here with my gut achin', I can hardly walk — and you're mad because I won't play chess."

"What do you think my gut feels like?"

I watched him turn and start down the aisle. He meant well, I knew. I gathered up the set. "Caribou — wait up!" I yelled.

Sometime later we finished the first lesson: learning how to place individual pieces on the board, and how to make a few opening gambits. Gee told me to never play the game unless I played to win. Never play any game to lose, particularly chess.

We sat back to rest.

This was the best time of day, Gee said. No Japs around yelling, bashing, trying to prove something. Time to talk. "One has to talk to get a reflection of who one is by seeing how the other guy reacts, don't you agree?"

"I suppose. I never thought much about it."

"There are three forces at work here," Gee observed, drawing a triangle on the ground with a stick. "Like legs of a triangle. First, food. Either we have enough or we're dead. Second, health. That needs no explanation. Third, attitude, which is probably the best medicine. Food, health, attitude. They're interlocked, each totally dependent on the other. We have to have all three. No food, no health. Bad attitude: the triangle collapses."

"You trying to tell me something?"

Gee smiled. "You're improving. At least you're off your butt." He nodded toward the bamboo barracks. "Those guys who turn in early, they're the ones I worry about."

"What are you, your brother's keeper?"

"Don't I wish."

"Then you're bucking for sainthood."

"Not a chance. Maybe I'm just selfish. If morale goes to pot, we all go."

I looked out at the blackness of jungle closing in like a dark shroud. I shivered and pushed a chunk of wood on the coals. Men were doing things to boost morale — their own, mostly: Fred Quick, Jim Ewing, and I had started a singing trio in Batavia, going around imitating the Ink Spots. Otto Schwarz, James Bergen, James Musto, and John Ferguson from New Jersey had done a hilarious imitation of the Dead End Kids. Perhaps it was time to start those things again in this camp, despite how lousy we felt. We needed it now more than ever.

Perhaps Gee was right about the third leg of the triangle.

On our first day off we went around from one group to another, singing. I sang bass, making an ass of myself deliberately, doing the talking parts to "We Three," "If I Didn't Care," and other Ink Spot tunes. And Gee and I spent a part of the day playing chess — a treat, moving pieces in daylight.

A group of onlookers gathered. It became strangely quiet. A shadow fell across the board, and we looked up into the face of a smiling guard. We stood up so quickly to salute we turned over the board, scattering the pieces.

"Chess-kah?" the guard smiled.

"Yes. We play chess," Gee said.

"I wish to learn chess," the guard said, smiling. He pointed at me. "You, me — play chess?"

"Uh — okay, sure," I said.

The guard had no rifle. He got down on his hands and knees and helped us pick up the chess pieces, sucking his gums, grinning like a friendly pup.

"You speak English?" I asked.

The guard produced a little pocket-sized translation book from his pocket. "I speak little bit English," he laughed. "We play chess. Okay-kah?"

F. H. "Pinky" King was one of the onlookers. "Be careful," he warned as we set up the pieces. "Don't beat th' little bastard."

I won in five moves, using the classic fool's mate.

My opponent stood up, bowed, and sucked his gums, and of

course I rose to my feet and bowed right back at him, wondering what would happen next.

"Thank you, thank you. One more, please," the guard smiled.

We set up the pieces again, and once more I was advised to lose. "Share the wealth," Gee said, frowning, shaking his head.

"That's not how you taught me to play the game," I reminded him.

I beat the guard again. This time in seven moves.

Again he wanted to play "one more" game.

After the third defeat, he bowed and, sweating profusely, marched away without so much as a look in our direction.

Pinky slowly wagged his head. "You've done it. You've caused him to lose face."

I felt uneasy about it. But as days went by, that incident was overshadowed by another that was potentially much more dangerous, or so it seemed at the time.

Rails arrived from the north on flatcars held on by two steel cables, one around the leading ends, a second around the tail ends, both fastened underneath the flatcar frame. More rails meant more work, more pressure from the guards, more beatings. Aside from that, we had the unwritten, seldom mentioned, three-word objective: sabotage, sabotage, sabotage — slow the railroad construction wherever, whenever, however possible.

Pinky King had been with a work party north of camp filling in gravel around crossties. He had seen the load of rails move in on a siding. That night he came to me with an idea.

"Good lord!" I said.

"What's th' matter, you yellow?"

"Damned right!"

"All this is gonna take is a little luck."

"Yeah. And the balls of an elephant!"

"You goin', or not?"

"Why me?"

"Because I'm askin' you, that's why."

"Good lord," I muttered.

Minutes later I was in the Japanese tool shack, of all places, fishing around in moonlight that seeped in through an open doorway, trying to lay my hands on a pair of wire cutters. "Good lord,"

I kept muttering to myself, glancing up every few seconds to make sure Pinky was still by the doorway watching for guards.

My hands eventually closed on the cutters. I grabbed them and eased toward the doorway just in time to hear Pinky hiss "Guard! Stay back!" and to see him stride away to the slit trench no more than two dozen steps away, according to plan, to divert the guard's attention.

He squatted across the trench with his pants down, and I pulled back in the shadow. The guard paused at the doorway and looked in. I felt my heart pounding up in my throat. I could smell the soap the man had used with his bath. I tried not to breathe. A century later he moved on, and I stood there, gasping — holding on to the door frame to keep from passing out. "Good lord," I muttered.

"Come on, we're wasting time!" Pinky said. "Now for the fun!"

"You're an idiot! You know that, don't you?"

We waited until the two guards patrolling the periphery of the compound stopped to talk to each other a substantial distance away. We crawled under the strands of barbed wire, staying on our hands and knees until a line of trees loomed between us and the camp. We galloped along the roadbed, then, staying up on our tiptoes, braced to jump for cover. "This is the craziest thing I've ever done in my life," I said.

"Yeah, ain't it great!" Pinky grinned.

We cut only one of the steel cables, the one at the south end of the flatcar. I started to toss the cutters into a tangle of underbrush.

"Good Lord NO!" Pinky hissed. "If they find 'em missin' they'll know the prisoners did it! We're takin' 'em back!"

It was bad enough on the nerves, stealing the tool; it was even worse returning it.

Eventually, we were back on our sleeping shelves. "Where th' hell have you been?" Gee asked.

"Out," Pinky chortled.

"Of our minds," I added.

We agreed not to place the burden of secrecy on anyone. So we never revealed what we had done, particularly after what we learned the following day.

During the night, twenty Japanese guards and engineers came in on a caboose pulled by a truck designed to take the place of a railroad locomotive. They were on their way to a camp farther south, and for some reason, their caboose was coupled to the north end of the flatcar with rails.

On the way south into camp that morning the untied ends of the rails came down, jamming into the ground. They were hurled — actually aimed by that second cable — and driven like giant spikes all the way through the front to the back walls of the caboose, some poking through the sides. At least five occupants were impaled and killed instantly. Others died later on, and a few were badly maimed. Few escaped without injury.

By the time Pinky's work party got there that morning, the Japanese had cleaned up most of the carnage. But he saw the caboose and what the rails had done to it; and he also saw the bodies laid out along the track. They must have thought it was an accident.

He told me about it later that evening. "I suppose we should pat ourselves on the back. But I shore didn't plan on that caboose."

"Are you sorry we did it?" I asked.

"I sure didn't plan no killin' like that."

A few days later, one of two guards with my work party was the guard I had beaten at chess.

Work progressed without incident. As darkness approached we headed back toward camp carrying sledge hammers and long-handled shovels along a narrow path that led past a small pond. There had to be leeches in the pond, but we were sweaty, dirty, and tired, and we talked the guards into letting us stop long enough to take quick baths.

I hung my shirt and shorts on the lower branches of a tree, as the others did. When we came out of the water the shirt was gone.

"Okay, joke's finished. Where's my shirt?" I asked.

No one apparently knew.

I had a premonition of trouble as we approached camp. There were outdoor racks that held tools by the tool shack, where hammers and shovels were kept. We couldn't see them until we were right upon them, and when they came into view my heart skipped a beat. There, waving like a flag, was my shirt.

My instinct was to go on by, to not look at the shirt, to not reach out and touch it. But it was the only one I had. I needed it.

I reached out to grab it.

"*Kodah!*" the guard screamed.

Guards grabbed me and shoved me against the tool shack. I was ordered to stand there.

A dozen steps away, three guards began checking their rifles, working the bolts. They left no doubt that I was in trouble.

Major Yamada stood before me. "You trade with Burmese! You know penalty?"

"I did not trade with Burmese!" I said, feeling completely helpless.

Yamada barked commands. More guards came and were checking their rifles.

Suddenly, Lieutenant Lattimore was there. "What is this?" he asked. "They catch you trading with the natives?"

"No. That guy, the one I beat at chess a week or so ago, he says I traded —"

"Okay. I heard about that. Take it easy. Let me talk to them."

Lattimore confronted Yamada. They were talking calmly, and suddenly Yamada hit the little lieutenant with his fist, sending his glasses flying.

Lattimore picked up his glasses and confronted Yamada again, not raising his voice, but leaving no mistake about his determination. Yamada was taller, and as he struck him again he laughed. Still, Lattimore kept his composure, refusing to walk away.

Now there were six men with rifles. I could taste the dry powder in my mouth. My heart pounded. I felt like I wanted to run, but I was glued in place. I wanted to pray, yet my thoughts were jumbled. All I could see in my mind's eye was an image of my mother, cackling in shadows, toothless, sinister, her face the color of purple, her lips a fiery red . . .

Suddenly, Lattimore stood beside me, looking up. "It's all over. Go back to the barracks, Charlie. Don't look around. Don't run. Just get goin' and don't look back."

Someone threw my shirt at my feet. I reached down and picked it up and walked away. I would never know who tossed it.

We didn't play chess that evening. I lay on my part of the shelf looking up into the dark eaves.

"Wanna talk about it?" Gee asked.

I shook my head. "Nothing to talk about."

"Well, suit yourself. But if you wanna talk —"

"Nothing to talk about," I insisted.

"I worry about guys like you."

I realized I owed my life to Lattimore. The lieutenant's sleeping mat was at the other end of the barracks. When he saw me coming he was grinning. "How do you feel?"

"I'm okay. Sir, I want to thank you."

"That's okay."

"I want you to know, when I first saw you in Batavia I wasn't too impressed. I —"

"You don't need to explain anything. We were lucky. Yamada knew that guard was telling a lie just to get even with you. I didn't have to work very hard to convince him."

"But he knocked you flat of your can! He could have killed you!"

"Kill an officer? Not likely. You, well, as I said, we were lucky."

I found Doc Hekking sitting on his bunk, winding pieces of cloth for bandages, too busy to look up. "You want something?"

"I don't know. I —"

"Well, speak up if you want something. Otherwise, as you see, I am busy."

"I guess I'm scared, Doc."

"Yes? Well, so am I. So are the others. It is okay."

"No, I mean real scared. Shook up. Damned near ready to fold my tent."

"So much slang. Texan is worst language in the world."

"I'm not a Texan. I'm from Kansas."

"Texas. Kansas. Same thing. I never learn Texan. Listen. Sit down. I tell you something."

I sat across from him.

He put his hand on my shoulder and looked me straight in the eyes. No man since a principal of high school, J. B. Garrison, had ever made me feel I was worthy of that much effort, and as I recall, when J. B. did it he was bawling me out.

"I saw what happened," Doc said. "You have great courage, you and Lieutenant Lattimore."

"Not me," I said. "I was never so scared in my life!"

"You did not show it. Listen. You must remember the fine

country you and Lattimore have. United States of America. It is wonderful country. It expects much, but you know it will give much too. It will never forget that you are prisoner, and one day, your people will come for you. It is your United States, but it is mine, too, and it is country of all people who want this thing, this hope, this dream we have. Soon the war is over. Your country, England, Australia, my country, my Netherlands — we will win. I know we will win because it is meant that men be free. We cannot lose, if we keep this courage. Others depend on us. We depend on each other. It is like a chain. You a link, me a link, all of us little links, you see?"

15

Test of Steel

"We're doing a slow-down. Tomorrow, first thing," Gee announced that morning. "Pass the word."

Looking along the sleeping shelf, he added, "At least we're still alive. Praise the Lord. Maybe it's the Doc's medicine."

"Medicine, or words. What do you know about rainy season?" I asked. "When does it start?"

"In May. Goes through October. It's not here yet. Let's take it one day at a time," Gee said.

We had the day off, and we found ourselves taking inventory. Some of us could reach around the upper part of our arms and touch the tips of our index fingers against the tips of our thumbs. Not unlike the others who had had dysentery, my ribs protruded, even those in my back. Most of us looked like skeletons, while a few had beriberi and were bloated. Apparently, I had a mild case of pellagra. But maybe because of Doc's lemon-flavored leaves from the jungle, or because of the eggs stolen by Freddie Quick from the guard's kitchen, I felt no pains except those of hunger, and even those went away with the dirty rice and soup. That was also dangerous, feeling no pain, yet walking around, slowly starving.

Word of a special work slow-down attempt was always passed

around the day before it was to commence. Sometimes it took only one or two men to start it. Usually the slow-downs happened spontaneously, without anyone saying anything. No one ever tried to work diligently, or fast. One became an artist at appearing to work at normal speeds while actually doing as little as possible.

I never knew who issued orders for slow-downs. It didn't pay to know, in case they beat you to try to find out.

We were moving dirt, building the roadbed across a valley that particular morning. I was at the other end of a *yo-ho* pole with Packrat McCone. The line moved so slowly that we kept bumping into the two-man carriers ahead of and behind us. It was harder to walk at that pace with a load of dirt. But we felt compelled to do whatever we could to delay completion of the railroad. It was one of the only weapons we had.

Without exception, every prisoner was involved. The guards knew what was going on, but they also knew that unless they killed all of us there was little they could do about it. *"Hoi! Kodah! Isoge! Isoge!"* they yelled, using bamboo poles on our backs, serving only to make the line move even slower.

Between whacks of the poles, McCone and I talked, trying to shut out the events unfolding around us.

I could remember doing things I had done as a free person, but being free was becoming a dream of something that had never really happened. I told Packrat about my early days in Partridge, Kansas; about where I was when the war started in Europe. He told me about the loneliness of his life as a youth in Montana, growing up on his parents' ranch while his father was away most of the time in Washington, D.C., doing what United States senators had to do.

"He was a senator?"

"Yep."

"Gee whiz! And you're here? In this?"

As we talked I kept my eyes on the guards. Yamada stood at the top of the dirt fill, looking down upon us, his face clouded with rage.

No one realized that Yamada had come up with a plan to stop the slow-down. He had said nothing to us, so the word was out that we would continue to control the speed of work the following day.

It would be the same thing, taking dirt off the top of two hills, filling in the valley between, so we would be virtually in lock-step, making the slow-down easy to control.

McCone and I worked together again. And again we talked and talked, to keep our sanity. I confessed that in my every thought, my every dream, Japanese guards were standing with rifles just as now, watching my every move.

"It's the same with me," Packrat said. "What are you going to do when we get out of this mess?"

"Go back to college."

"Not me. I'm going as far back in th' hills as I can get."

"Where?"

"You know where. Montana, of course."

"Why?"

"To hunt. Live off the land. Be alone."

"I'm not into politics. But if your old man's a United States senator, why in hell are you here? You could be an officer, cooling your heels in Washington."

"Never wanted to be an officer. Too much responsibility."

"*Hoi! Kodah! Karnero,*" yelled a guard right behind us. The pole came down on Packrat's back. *"Isoge!"*

A few seconds later I turned to look back. "You okay?"

"Yeah. Just stings a little. Takes more'n that to hurt me."

In the gray of dawn Yamada stood on the hill above the point where digging was under way. He was watching the prisoners emerge ghostlike from the low area shrouded with fog. We could hear the sporadic yelling of guards far back in the haze, but no one could see what was going on back there. It must have angered him, watching his engineers happily working shoulder to shoulder with the "slaves," shoveling dirt — not because they had to, but because they wanted to serve the emperor. Yamada was trying to see the line farther back. There appeared to be nothing out of the ordinary as prisoners came into view, dropping their sacks to be loaded. But he had to have known.

As the sun came up and as fog lifted, it apparently struck him: the entire line was moving even slower than it had the day before.

He walked the few steps down onto the area that was being excavated. Lieutenant Matsuoko, stripped to the waist, was humming and working, obviously enjoying himself.

"Did you change the stakes?" Yamada asked, referring to markers set on the dirt fill to establish the daily quota.

Matsuoko stopped digging and bowed. "Good morning, Major! How are you this morning?"

"Did you change those stakes!" Yamada demanded.

"Hai! Of course, Major! The stakes are changed!" More bowing. More sucking of gums.

"Are those prisoners working slower than yesterday, or am I just imagining it?"

The fat little man wiped the sweat from his forehead, leaving a streak of mud. He adjusted his cap and leaned on the spade handle, his mouth open. He squinted, appearing to study the line of workmen coming across the valley like ants in slow motion. "Ah-h-h-h, so! Ah-h-h-h, so!" He studied Yamada from the corners of his eyes. "Perhaps a little slower. They are sore and stiff lately, Yamadasan. Perhaps it is the soreness and stiffness?"

Yamada glared at him. He turned and stalked down the hill to the nearest guard. The guard pulled himself to rigid attention.

"Are you watching these prisoners?" he bellowed.

"Hai! Hai!"

"Well, make them work faster! They are working much too slowly. Use that rifle as a club. Pass the word!"

"Hai! Wakara mas!"

Yamada found Sergeant Kosha strolling alone like a dolt, apparently doing nothing. "I am doing your work for you!" he shouted. "It is your job to keep these men moving — is it not so?"

"Hai! So it is, Major. However, Lieutenant Matsuoko and I agree that the prisoners are overtired. It is to be expected —"

Yamada slapped him in the face and stood glaring at him. He slapped him again to drive home his point. "Make the slaves work faster!" he said, and he stalked away.

He marched back to his place on the hill to watch, to make sure his orders were carried out.

McCone and I climbed the hill as slowly as we dared. It was almost mid-morning, time for the first rest break. Dozens of men had been beaten, but the line was still moving at a snail's pace. Pinky King and a frail kid named Frankie Adams were in front of us, the kid glancing around occasionally with a big grin and a knowing look. Yamada had taken up a new position near the men who were hacking at the roots of a gnarled tree, trying to get it to fall. We assumed he was absorbed at the moment with progress of the tree removal, until we saw him watching Frankie. We wanted to warn the frail marine. It was too late.

"You!" Yamada bellowed, pointing at Frankie. *"Kotchie ne koi!"*

Eyes filled with terror, Frankie dropped his end of the pole. He walked over and stood at attention in front of the major, his bony legs shaking.

"All men stop!" Yamada shouted, holding up his hand.

Like a giant centipede, the line gradually came to a halt, front part first. Far back in the valley, guards were still shouting. Men leaned on shovels. Sacks slid along on wires and dropped to the ground. Sunken eyes peered up from the valley. Finally, the whole world seemed to be listening.

"What is your name?" Yamada yelled at the pathetic skeleton in front of him.

"Franklin Adams. United States Marines —"

"Franklin Adams, were you asked to work more slowly?"

"No, sir," Frankie croaked.

"Were you told to work more slowly?"

Frankie was pale and shaking, but he said nothing as the major stood in front of him, hands on his hips, glaring at him. A shovel banged against a stone. Someone cleared his throat. I could feel my heart pumping in my neck, anger churning in my gut.

Yamada belted Frankie in the mouth. Blood trickled down the corners of his mouth, and Frankie began to sob.

"Answer my question!" Yamada roared.

"You bastard!" Frankie sobbed, wiping his mouth, looking at the blood on the back of his dirty hand.

"Stop that!" The shout came from the valley.

All eyes trained on the lone figure that was climbing the hill and yelling "Stop that, you cowardly sonuvabitch! Leave that boy alone!" It was Lattimore. The short stack of bones and guts. Mostly guts, the raw courage variety. "Ah'm the one who gave the order to slow the work. These men are exhausted. You're killing them, working them to death!"

Yamada grinned like a maniac. "Thank you, Lieutenant." He motioned to the guards who rushed to grab him. "I suspected you. I wondered if you had the courage to come forth."

Lattimore was beaten then. We didn't want to watch, yet our

eyes returned again and again to the sorry display of inhumanity. We had seen it before, time after time: the Japanese male in the role of master, venting his feelings of inferiority. This time we found ourselves closing in on this devil, this Yamada, without realizing what we were doing. Shots rang out above our heads. We drew back.

"Tell your men to work faster, Lieutenant!" Yamada screamed.

Lattimore said nothing.

Yamada knocked his glasses off. He kicked him in the stomach, crumpling him on the jagged rocks. He kicked him in the head.

Lattimore got up slowly, staggered, and fell. He got up again.

"Give it up, Lieutenant!" someone yelled. "What difference does it make?"

"Let's go, men," someone begged. "Move it out!"

Yamada heard the plea. He stood like a man quarried, watching Lattimore from the corners of his eyes. Great rivers of sweat soaked through the front and back of his shirt. Rifles were striking flesh behind us, poles raining down on bare backs and shoulders. We were moving, but Lattimore and Yamada were still locked in a battle of wills.

McCone and I moved out of sight without seeing what finally happened. The fact that the line moved may have saved enough face for Yamada. But it had to have been a hollow victory, for Yamada knew it was the prisoners who had resumed the flow of work, not so much because they feared him, but because they respected Lattimore.

The physical damage was bad for the lieutenant, even though they had beaten him many times before and he knew how to roll with the punches. Doc worked on him until late that night, patching him up the best he could, with words as much as with anything else. He had little else.

For many, survival became a matter of sheer will. One had to have luck, of course, and psychologically, depending on one's belief, one had to have squared things away between himself and his higher power. I knew no atheists in prison camp.

I prayed to Christ, the son of God, at first. Then I went directly to God Himself, never mind the intermediary. Somewhere along the way I remembered a line from a story about the near annihilation of the Armenians: "To the inexplicable, in us and above us." I wasn't sure what inexplicable meant, so I prayed to Christ, to God, to Buddha, to Mohammed, to Shinto — to anybody out there, over there, down there, up there, who might be listening. And I ended each prayer with the phrase "to the inexplicable, in us and above us, amen, so be it — give me back my freedom, Lord, and I'll do whatever you want me to do." Sure, I was trying to drive a bargain. I didn't realize that, later on, I would spend the rest of my life wondering what the Lord really wanted of me.

I began to think of freedom as something like the blank spot beyond the hill — something you knew was there, but something you could no longer see or clearly imagine. Even when we "escaped" temporarily to trade with the Burmese we never knew how far to trust them, so we made it quick, we said very little, we made our trade, and slipped quickly back to the comparative safety of camp.

There were fewer than a half dozen known instances when anyone actually tried to escape for good. For pitiful pieces of Burmese paper money, those who tried were betrayed and brought back by the Burmese. No one ever really made it. The Burmese were starving too. They had much to gain if you tried to escape and they caught you: the reward for your body, dead or alive, was a lot of money to them, whatever it was. For a person with white skin, the chances were nil.

Put simply, the Japanese controlled the land and sea for too many miles in all directions. In March 1943, we realized the frightening reality of this. Three Australians tried to make it north to India. It was not a knee-jerk decision to escape; it was the culmination of a well thought-out plan. They almost made it to the Indian border when they were captured by Burmese and brought back to Thanbyuzayat. I was one of those to witness their execution. It was to become one of my worst nightmares.

Before they killed them, the Japanese made it a point to give us a chance to talk to them, to learn how impossible the chances of escape were. "Don't try it, mates," one of the condemned Aussies said. "We almost starved to death. We couldn't sleep because of the living things what crawls and walks in the bloody night. And then them animals, them Chans. They was following, always waitin' for their bloody chance. It's no wonder the Nips are unconcerned about the fences around the camps. They ain't no place to go . . ."

They were made to dig their own graves. The soil was black and soft in Thanbyuzayat, and they dug them deep, taking their time.

They were made to stand near the edges in front of the holes as members of the firing squad approached to take their places. All three Aussies asked not to be blindfolded. A lieutenant drew his sword from its sheath. As he raised it high, sun glinting on the blade, I closed my eyes.

"Go ahead, you yellow-bellied bastards, get on with it!" one of them shouted, the words a final accusation.

One of the poor men dropped to his knees in front of his grave, and with his eyes closed, his hands clasped, he moved back and forth, back and forth, shaking, his lips moving. I had tried to keep my eyes shut. I couldn't.

They were shot in the face.

The lieutenant went to each one then with a Luger, a grim, half-scared look on his face. He sent a bullet into each man's skull. The smell of gunpowder drifted into our nostrils. The soldiers shoved the bodies, and they flopped into the holes like limp, dead animals.

My hands felt clammy. My stomach churned as we stood there, waiting to be dismissed.

The prisoners later talked about the bravery of the Aussies. There was no doubt about that. But all I could think about was having witnessed human beings at their sickest, lowest level.

We became aware of the fact that British intelligence forces were watching the progress of the railroad. We didn't know at the time that men under Maj. Orde Charles Wingate were operating in southern Burma, while at the same time Americans were destroying bridges behind enemy lines in northern Burma. The Americans were members of OSS 101 (Office of Strategic Services) out of Kunming, China. While no one of our group knew about OSS until after the war, a few of us talked to a man who said he was a member of a British intelligence unit — which presumably had to have been from Wingate's force — when we were at Kilo 40.

He actually had the gall to sneak into camp, spend a few hours talking with prisoners working on the dirt fill, then disappear into the jungle before roll call that evening. He blended in remarkably well, allowing only a few to know who he was. He said he had watched from a distance with binoculars and had decided to come on in for a closer look. We thought he was either suicidal or crazy, and of course we went to great effort not to give him away. It was an enormous boost to morale to know that an Allied intelligence unit was close by. But at the same time it was depressing to learn that this man's outfit would not attempt to take us to freedom. It would be easy, parachuting in to liberate the camps, he said, but considering our physical state, trying to take us out on a long march would risk getting us all killed.

The Japanese brought Koreans in to supplement the guard force. They wore the same uniforms, but were easily identified by shooting-star patches sewn onto the upper left sides of their jackets and shirts. The insignia designated them as occupation forces. They were larger physically than the Japanese, evidently picked because of their size. They appeared to hate the Japanese guards and prisoners alike; to despise themselves. Their dispositions were usually sour, and we were quick to hang the same label on all of them: they were mean and not to be trusted. Like the Japanese, they were emotional and high-strung, capable of inflicting pain without warning. The Koreans and Japanese frequently fought among themselves, resorting to jujitsu, the objective always to cause the opponent's anger and superior strength to work against him.

We were acutely aware of how powerless we were to help ourselves; we knew how little it would take to bring on the full wrath of the "masters."

I was beaten with a rifle because I had not moved quickly enough when an engineer yelled "Speed-o." The guard first made me stand down in a trench so his face was even with mine. He hit me with his fists until blood from my face was on his hand and tasted warm in my mouth. Then he made me bow and salute him. He didn't like the way I did that, so he picked up his rifle, walked around behind where I couldn't see or anticipate the blow, then struck me in the back with the butt end. It felt like it broke something in my back, although x-rays since the war never confirmed it. The pain was severe for several weeks. My spirits sank to a new low.

On March 10, we were moved from Kilo 25 to Kilo 35. We were moved again March 20 from Kilo 35 to Kilo 14.

And we heard the best and possibly the worst news in almost a year: Thanbyuzayat was bombed. A few prisoners were killed. Some were maimed.

The British said it was an American bomber, the Americans said it was British. What difference? It was a freakish mistake, of course, but the camp was bombed and machine-gunned from the air — proving on the positive side that the Allies now had sufficient strength to fly a bomber that far, and on the negative side that they didn't know they were killing prisoners.

So much for hopes and dreams of repatriation, we thought.

Lieutenant Lattimore went to Doc Hekking with an idea. I was inside the barracks. I don't believe either men knew I was listening.

Supplies of food were still woefully inadequate, and Lattimore was desperate.

"Doc, they take you outside for plants of medicinal value. Is there anything out there with food value?"

Doc looked around to make sure no one could hear. "Truthfully, not much. There are weeds that look and taste a bit like vegetables. They provide chlorophyll, the thing that gives color to plants."

"Do you think it would be worthwhile, bringing some of them in to thicken the soup?"

"Yes, of course! It would be good for us!"

"Really?"

"Of course! Of *course!*"

So they started bringing in sacks full of weeds which the men assumed were vegetables. I never said anything. Some of the prisoners may have known more than they let on. I don't know.

The weeds did make the soup thicker, adding the appearance of extra nutrition. They didn't hurt anyone; nor did the occasional python or cobra, which had been caught, dressed and thrown in along with the weeds. Or the stray cat, or dog, or water buffalo blood. Anything with nourishment, real or imagined, helped.

But despite the best efforts of the cooks, Lattimore, and Doc Hekking, the lineups for sick calls steadily lengthened.

With fewer men on the job, there was greater distress for Yamada, who feared that his part of the railroad effort was falling hopelessly behind. He raved and ranted. And he gave Henri an ultimatum: no more than ten percent of the men could be kept in camp because of sickness.

"Men do not get sick by quota," Henri told him. "They get sick because you starve them and give them no medicine. How can I convince you of that?"

"Japanese have no food."

"Japanese eat well! I see you! I see you!"

Yamada slapped him across the face. "You are no good doctor! *Pokaro!*" he screamed.

That night, I heard Fitzsimmons telling Doc to be careful.

But the next morning Doc kept twenty-five prisoners, mostly Americans, in from work. And again Yamada sent for him. I stayed out of sight, but I got close enough to listen.

Doc stood at attention in front of Yamada's desk.

"You defy my order! Why do you disobey me? Am I to treat you like common soldier?"

"Twenty-five men are sick," Doc said.

"You are a fool!" Yamada growled.

He ordered Doc to take off his shirt. He had the guard strike him once across the back with a bamboo pole.

Doc winced, but he didn't make a sound.

"Why do you risk your life for worthless Americans?" Yamada asked. "Send five more men to work and I will let you go."

Doc glared at him. "You are an animal! You are a coward!"

The major nodded his head to the guard, and the pole came down on Doc's back five more times.

When they let him leave, oddly they did not force any of the twenty-five sick men out on the road.

But this became Yamada's standing order: for each man above the ten percent quota, Doc would be struck one blow, harder some mornings than others, depending on which guard wielded the pole. After three days, Henri's back was black and blue and he could not bear to lie on it.

Still he would not relent. Nor would Yamada.

All of the other officers, Australians and Americans alike, tried to convince Doc that the camp commander would kill him before he would give in. "No, he will not have me killed," Doc said. "He will hurt me, but kill me? I do not think so. The Japanese need me too."

"But why are you doing it?" Fitzsimmons asked him after one particularly brutal beating.

"I am not dead, you see," Doc reminded him. "If I give in, the sick will be the ones to die. And there will be many more sick when rainy season comes. They must not be allowed to get in the habit of sending everyone to the railroad."

"But what if they kill you?" Fitzsimmons asked. "What good will that do?"

"I am a doctor. It is my duty to help the sick. Do you deny it is my duty?"

"If they kill you, how will we make it without you?" Fitzsimmons asked.

Doc grinned. "Go away, please. I am busy man."

By late April we had changed camps twice more, moving from Kilo 14 to Kilo 25 (staying briefly in the same camp we had been in earlier) and then from Kilo 25 to Kilo 45 on May 2, 1943. We were in Kilo 18 from May 14 to July 24, and were brought back to Kilo 30.

The Japanese appeared to be using our group as a kind of utility force, to finish off a roadbed here, add crossties and rails there, help with bridges, or go back to a camp to finish off a segment started and for some reason abandoned by another work party. It was odd, the way they sometimes removed a work force before an assignment was completed. The reason behind this action was a mystery until we were taken to Kilo 80.

From the outset we had an eerie feeling about that move. There was something strange about the way the guards acted long before we got there. And then came the first whiff of what was wrong: the unmistakable smell of death. It hung there in heavy stillness, a sickening smell, offending the senses.

As we approached the camp, the smell grew stronger.

16

The Rain Came

The sickening smell hung in the air as we arrived in Kilo 80 on September 11.

We pulled up to the main gate, riding in the backs of trucks. Before we could jump off, Lattimore asked the guard riding on top of the cab to keep us in formation until he and two other prisoners and guards went to investigate. They took two shovels.

Soon, Lattimore was back for more men, more shovels. From the look on his face we knew that whatever he had seen had to be horrible.

Four of us grabbed shovels and went with him out back to the remains of human bodies — a mass grave poorly covered, huge blue flies swarming around arms, legs, heads and torsos, the flesh partly rotted. Armies of ants crawled through eyes and noses. An old Burmese man stood near the edge of the clearing, pointing, a crazed look in his eyes. "Plague," he cried. "Plague."

We gagged again and again, but we finished covering the parts.

Before we settled into the buildings, we poured boiling water over all of the sleeping spaces.

Two men trying to catch a rat were told that the animal might

152

be a carrier of plague. There was nothing to remotely resemble panic, although we reached a new plateau of apprehension. Yamada finally informed us: two weeks prior to our arrival, 500 Burmese workers — everyone at the camp — had died with cholera.

The rain came at last.

It started with a gentle roar across the jungle that morning, then it gained momentum, building to a roaring crescendo across the trees, sending torrents of water under sleeping shelves inside the barracks, turning the aisles into rivers. The creek out back overflowed, disgorging itself in the river that ran beneath the railroad. The river rose beneath the bridge. The roofs leaked. There was no way now to fix them.

Like isolated pizzicato in the midst of a powerful symphony, a scattering of mail came trickling in — letters from families in the United States. They brought the first words from home; the first confirmation we were human and missed after all. We realized now that people in the United States knew there were survivors of the *Houston,* and as of the moment, they knew we were alive.

The Red Cross had sent the letters via Bangkok. They were reduced to telegrams: "I hope you are well. We are fine. Your friend, Bob Anderson, sends his best. Love, Mom." That was my letter. We had permission to reply using phrases "recommended" by the Japanese. Most men wrote. I was one of the few who didn't. Why write when the odds were against survival? What would one say — "Hello Mom. I am well. I hope you are too. See you soon!" ? Who were we kidding?

Rainy season had become serious, and almost everyone in camp was sick. Five men had already died in Kilo 80:

William F. Mattfield
F. W. Brothers
William H. Dickens
Caston Pitts
James R. Wilson

What were the odds for the rest of us?

Jim Evans didn't care, but my mother did, so why write to her and build up her hopes? Better to wait until I was out of Japanese hands, I decided.

Gee became sick again. And this time it looked as though nothing would save him. Doc could not determine what caused him to have such a constant and high fever. It was baffling: unlike any type of malaria he had ever treated.

He had an ampule of sulfa Fitzsimmons had "purchased" from friendly natives in Kun Knit Kway, promising them that the government of the United States would eventually pay them. The sulfa might work, Doc said, if it were properly formulated. He had no way of knowing whether it was or not, unfortunately, so there was high risk if he used it.

Gee realized the quandary. "What are my chances?" he asked through clenched teeth.

Doc shrugged. "We must do something, you see? But there is a fifty percent chance it is no good."

"And a fifty percent chance it is okay? So what are we waitin' for?" Gee said.

Doc gave him the injection and stayed with him for the rest of the day and night.

Gee responded the following day. "Well, whattaya know?" he beamed. "We made it!"

Shortly after that, Doc found what he had searched for since first entering the Burma jungle: a pomelo tree, with fruit like grapefruit, though much larger. What interested him most was not the fruit but the gray-colored substance on its skin: the fungus, or mold, the kind his grandmother had used so successfully.

In camp he scraped the mold off into a mess tin, saving every particle as though it were pure gold. He diluted some of it in plain water to make a paste. The mold was called *pipijan* by the Javanese, meaning "little penny." It was a powerful antibiotic which worked miraculously on scratches and cuts, preventing and curing infections. It could also cure diphtheria, meningitis, and tetanus. (It would be 1945 before a hospital in Bangkok found that this mold was a form of penicillin, not unlike the antibiotic discovered in 1928 by the famous English bacteriologist Sir Alexander Fleming and made widely available in 1943.)

Doc tried using maggots once to clean out skin ulcers. He retrieved them from a slit trench and placed them in one of Packrat's tin cans, which had tiny holes poked in the bottom so that water could be poured over them. He applied the maggots by dipping them out with a spoon and placing them directly into sores containing pus. It was painless while the grublike larvae were eating away the pus, but when the pus was gone, the soft-bodied critters continued eating into the unaffected flesh, and the pain was excruciating until they were removed. They were then scraped out with the spoon. The main problem with this process was that it was too slow. Doc did not use the maggots again, although some of the men with stronger stomachs continued using them on their own sores.

Doc had discovered on one of his infrequent trips to the Thanbyuzayat "hospital" that a British doctor was using maggots as a source of protein, fishing them out of slit trenches at night, washing them, then working with cooks sworn to secrecy to get them into the soup at night without the men knowing it. They may have provided a minimum amount of protein, but Doc Hekking never thought they were worth the risk. There was no way he felt he could get them clean enough to put in food. So he never tried.

I was lying on the shelf with malaria the morning of the saber incident. By lantern light the men had just filed out through the gate to work, and Doc and Slug were starting to make their rounds of the sick.

"You, doctor!" Yamada shouted from the barracks entrance. They stopped and turned around.

"You say seventy-five men too sick to work?"

"Yes, Major," Doc said. "Malaria and dysentery, mostly."

"I will inspect the sick."

"As you wish," Doc said.

A guard brought a lantern and fell in behind the three men.

Yamada stopped at the foot of the man who lay right next to me. He drew his saber and placed the tip of the blade on the outer surface of the man's gut. The man stiffened, a horrified look on his face.

"You sick?" Yamada asked, lips curled in a vicious grin.

The man nodded, obviously too scared to speak.

Yamada pushed the skin in with the blade. "Too sick to work?"

Sweat popped out on the man's face. He shot out from under the blade and sat up.

"*Horyo* not sick!" Yamada screamed, whacking him across the shoulder with the flat side of the blade. He drew the saber back as if he would stab him. "You! Outside! You work!"

The man trotted toward the end of the building where another guard was waiting with a lantern.

By some miracle Yamada passed me by and went to the man four places down.

I watched in the gathering daylight, peeking out through the atap sides of the building. Only twenty-five men were left on the shelves by the time Yamada had gone through all four buildings.

"You see, Doctor, you lie! You no good doctor!" he shouted.

Doc, Slug, and I stood helplessly by, watching the sick men being prodded out through the gate and down toward the valley.

Doc was taken into the guard room then, and we counted twenty whacks. They had stripped him to the waist as they had before, and this time the flesh on his back was like a piece of bloody meat.

"I am told it will be the same each morning again, unless I stay within the quota," Doc said when he finally came outside.

"What do you plan to do?" Slug asked.

"Be a doctor —"

"This time, they'll kill you for sure!" Slug warned.

"No, I don't think so. He needs a doctor now more than ever."

To try to save Doc, some went to work when all they could do was lie on the ground beside the track and toss gravel between the ties. Some urged others to carry them to work. But even then, there were never enough men on the job to satisfy Yamada's quota. Even Lieutenant Lattimore was sick. One evening he walked as far as the bamboo pole separating Doc's "sick bay" from the rest of the barracks. He stumbled and passed out, falling flat on his face. He had malaria. Doc gave him one of the last doses of liquid quinine. Two days later the fever broke, and a few days after that he was back on his feet helping others.

We became our brothers' keepers, doing things for one another we had never dreamed of doing. There was no choice.

Everywhere one looked, men were caring for one another, washing feces and vomit from bamboo beds, taking drinking water to someone, bathing a man's forehead with a damp cloth, doing whatever could be done to bring comfort and hope.

I found myself helping a man who had soiled his bedding, not thinking twice about cleaning the bamboo poles upon which he slept, bathing his buttocks, using a part of a shirt and boiled water cooled in a section of bamboo. I sat with him for three evenings after work. I wondered why I couldn't weep when he died. He couldn't have been more than twenty-three. I felt sorry for him. I felt sorry for his parents or girlfriend or for whoever loved him — but I couldn't weep. I could not relate to the man, or I wouldn't. I knew I was selfish being so concerned about myself, thankful that I was the one alive, and I hated myself for having such thoughts. To make matters worse, my body ached. I knew I still had malaria, and I was quite aware that no man was immortal.

Assuming I was the dead man's close friend, the guards ordered me to take charge of a four-man burial party the following day. I waited until the body stiffened so it would be easier to carry. We used two rice sacks, bringing one down over the dead man's head all the way to his waist; pulling the other up from his feet, tying the tops of the bags where they met. I caught one of the others eyeing me as I took the man's clothing and shoes and put them by my own things.

"You have a problem with that?" I asked.

"I need those shoes." He looked at me then looked away, as though this was too painful to talk about.

"See if they fit you," I said, shoving them toward him.

"Doesn't matter if they fit or not. I've got a native lined up who will give me a bunch of food for shoes. I'm starving."

I looked into sunken eyes. What could I say? "Take 'em. And good luck," I said.

We dug the grave beside a fallen log, mindful we were close to a nest of scorpions. It was rocky soil. We couldn't go down beyond a foot or two.

We stood there as Lattimore, tears glistening in his eyes, said some nice things about the man, a soldier from his outfit. Even the Japanese showed respect, standing at attention, saluting when we lowered the body. I helped shovel dirt to cover the guy, being careful not to let stones drop on his face beneath the sack, feeling dizzy, barely able to see. Someone helped me back to the barracks.

I shook with chills and fever that night. All day the next day and for two days more I could hear in the valley the men working on the bridge, pulling on lines raising a boom then dropping it, raising the boom then dropping it on top of the long timbers driven deep in the ground. *"Ich-e nee no san-yo; ich-e nee no san-yo,"* the chant went, hour after hour, day after day, the boom hitting the timber each time on the last syllable. They had used elephants to bring the timbers in from the jungle, and they were sticking timbers in the ground to support horizontal members and crossties and rails. It was the end. There was nothing beyond that bridge. Only death. Nothing but a blank.

It was as though every man in camp knew it.

Fitzsimmons, Lattimore, and Doc got together — not far enough away from where I lay, because I would have preferred not to hear.

They must have thought I was too far gone to care one way or the other. "Something has to be done to save the men from drowning in their own depressions," I heard Fitzsimmons say. The question was what, and how. Time was running out. Either they did something now, or soon it would be too late.

The three officers sat in the dark talking, trying to figure out what to do.

"I have only one more thing I can try," I heard Doc say. That was all I heard. I must have gone to sleep after that.

Someone had to have talked Yamada into an extra day off, because all of the men were in camp.

"What's going on?" I asked Bird Dog.

"Never mind. Get this slop down your gullet before you kick th' bucket."

"But I'm not hungry."

"Don't gimme that crap. Open wide, buster."

What Bird Dog had in the spoon was the same old watery soup and dirty rice. And then came something else. Two white pills.

"Quinine?" I asked.

"Yep. Down the hatch."

I didn't study the pills carefully before I put them in my mouth and swallowed them. "Where'd you get 'em? I thought we were out of quinine ages ago."

"We were."

"Then where did you get 'em?"

"From Packrat."

"Good God. He trade for 'em?"

"He made 'em."

"Good lord!"

The rain let up, the sun went in and out of the clouds, and Bird Dog said, "Come on, Charlie. Up on your feet. The Doc wants to talk to us."

"About what?"

"How th' hell do I know? Says it's about some important instructions."

It was steamy and hot, and we came to gather under trees in the shade. We could see the bridge in the valley, rails snaking toward it, glistening in the sun. Guards stood by saying nothing, rifles across their bellies. And the men stood or squatted on haunches or sat wherever they could, on logs, on stumps, on the ground, not knowing what to expect.

"Boys, I must tell you something," Doc began. Leaves rustled in the trees. Someone cleared his throat. The talking dwindled to silence. "You will be going home one day very soon, now," Doc said. "I must warn you, since I will not be with you to tell you what to eat or how to take care of yourselves once you are home. It will not be the same with you as with other people. You cannot eat like other people. Your stomachs, they are not big, you see? How you say — they have shrunk. So you must take it easy on food.

"When you get home, do not eat two eggs for breakfast every morning, as I know many of you did in the past. Two eggs are very bad for you. One egg, that is fine. You eat only one egg a day. And do not eat just beef. Eat fish and chicken, because they are better for you . . ."

I couldn't believe what I was hearing.

It was not "if" we would make it home, it was "when." There was not the slightest doubt in Doc's voice or manner. We *were* going home, and that was that.

"Doc, you heard some news?" someone asked.

Doc was ignoring the question.

"Be quiet!" another man hissed. "Guards have big ears."

It was taken for granted that Doc had a private pipeline to news — possibly, a line directly Upstairs.

That evening, Gee and Bird Dog came "to share the good cheer." They stood in the mud, rain spattering on their backs. I lay stomach down on the bamboo shelf, face toward the aisle.

"You hear what th' Doc said?" Bird Dog asked.

"I heard him," I said. "Either he's the best actor in the world, or he actually believes what he's saying."

"You believe him, don't you?"

I looked deep into Bird Dog's eyes. I saw a reflection of my own concerns. "I'd like to believe him."

"Maybe he heard some news," said Caribou.

"What news?" I asked. "This is January; they've had us for almost two years, and except for that one air raid on Thanbyu-zayat, we've seen no signs of anyone. I don't know where Doc gets his news, or even if he does. Maybe they've forgotten us. Maybe we're already dead and we don't know it."

The silence between us lasted several seconds.

"They're out there," Caribou said, finally. "I feel it in my bones. We're goin' home, folks, just like th' man said."

"Damned right," said Page.

"Tell you what," said Caribou. "Why don't th' three of us make ourselves a pact, what do you say? Like, why don't we get ourselves a little ole piece of land and start a ranch in Texas when we get back?"

"What the hell makes you think I'd live in Texas? I'm from Kansas, remember?"

"Because Texas is the best state for a ranch!"

"Yeah," said Bird Dog. "Karuthers. Man, that's th' town."

"Ka — what?" asked Caribou.

"You heard me."

"Never heard tell of no Ka-ruther — whatever th' hell —"

"Karuthers, birdbrain!"

"Okay, okay," I said. "We'll take Texas. Karuthers. Who cares, as long as it's in the United States. So how much money are we going to have to have?"

"Maybe a thousand bucks apiece, to get ourselves a pretty good spread t'start out with," Caribou said. "That includes a bull and a coupla heifers."

"We'll need a barn," said Bird Dog. "Forget a house. After livin' in this, we can live anywhere for a coupla years 'till we get th' herd started."

"Yeah, forget th' house," said Caribou. "We'll need a rooster and three hens, so each of us will have an egg apiece for breakfast . . ."

"And a coupla hogs for bacon."

"One of those heifers better be a milk cow," I suggested. "It's gonna take a lot of milk."

"Better make that two milk cows," said Caribou. "Lordy me! You know something, folks? I can see us eatin' a cow and a bull jest for breakfast one mornin'!"

"Gonna be fun, ain't it?" Bird Dog chortled.

And the two of them laughed.

They laughed while rain roared in the trees, belting in sheets along the flimsy atap roof, soaking those who were attempting to sleep on the shelves.

They laughed as they stood in mud and slosh; intoxicated with hope, confidence radiating from one to the other, the momentum of strength building — all borne out of believing in something they could neither see nor hear nor touch nor prove.

And I found myself sharing the great insanity, enveloped with the heady feeling we were going to make it.

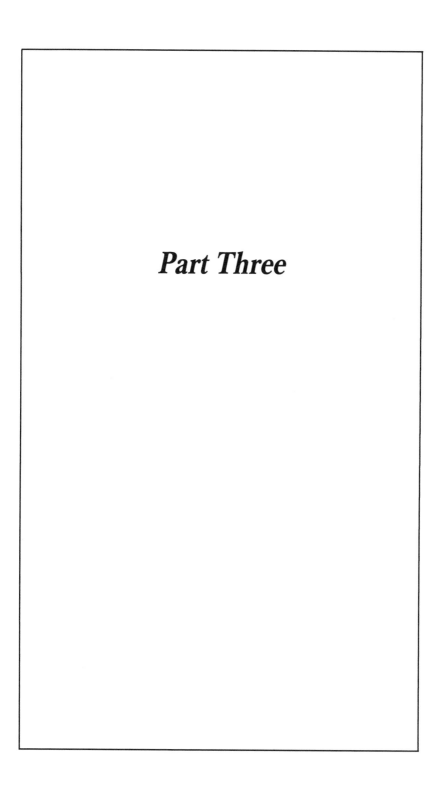

Part Three

17

The Last Man Out

Not long after Doc's one-egg-a-day talk — mass hypnotism, I'm sure of it now — I was back at work. The malaria had either reached the end of its cycle, or something else had happened. It was strange how much better I felt.

We were working with a cleanup party on the bridge at Kilo 114 on January 9 when Yamada announced that the railroad project was completed — finished on time, he said. He was wrong. It was actually two months behind schedule.

It was steamy and miserable as Yamada stood on the bridge looking down upon us, speaking as though he had completed the entire project himself. He even led a scattered applause, grinning idiotically as though we could share in the joy of his triumph. An elephant roared disapproval in the middle of his speech, and we couldn't restrain our laugh.

We were moved out of Kilo 114 the next day and put into a fenced-in area resembling a corral. We were sorted into three groups: one would go to Japan; one to Saigon, French Indochina; another to stay and maintain the railroad.

The Japanese lieutenant who supervised the sorting was nervous and irritable and didn't appear to know what he was doing. He fumbled and squinted at lists of prisoners' names, and there appeared to be no logic to the way he made selections. A little Japanese guard friendly to the Americans passed the word that we would be body-searched (stripped to the skin) before we left the fenced-in area — as if anyone had anything to hide. As it developed, someone did: Frank Torp of the 131st had kept a diary, complete with dates, hidden among his belongings. Another soldier was on his way to the hospital, and Frank had already slipped the diary to the man, keeping only the dates written on scraps of paper hidden inside his shirt. The diary was confiscated. But by some miracle the friendly Japanese guard was assigned to search Torp, and when he saw the paper he grinned and ignored it.

We were told for the first time who would be going where, even though we would not actually be taken there until several weeks later. Then we were loaded onto flatcars and shipped southeast into Thailand, crossing the Kwai River on the largest bridge we had seen in the jungle. We spent several hours with the British who had built the incredible crossing. "It's a kind of bloody monument," said a grinning, bedraggled British soldier. "Our C.O.'s idea of stalling the railroad, actually. You know: spend an inordinate amount of time on one bridge, slow completion of the entire project."

A British colonel had succeeded in talking a Japanese major into building a monument that "would last a thousand years" with his name engraved on it. It was a first-rate idea, using the Japanese major's ego to slow completion of the railroad. But it was not likely that that was what had slowed completion of the railroad. Others also helped, like those in Black Force, working as slowly as they dared. And sickness and death among workers played the greatest role.

We were moved into Camp Three, Kanchanaburi, Thailand, the evening of January 12, 1944. A few days later, an American bomber came down low to knock out the Japanese antiaircraft guns around the Kwai River Bridge. A day or two after that, a British bomber did a number on the bridge itself. Even this did little to delay use of the railroad. The bridge was quickly repaired, and the Japanese started moving troops across it.

What was left of the 194 Americans of Black Force and the 590 Australians who had been in Batavia together were reunited in the huge Kanchanaburi camp just outside of Bangkok. We compared notes. We learned that in the fourteen months on the railroad, nineteen percent of our men were dead. No one came through unscathed.

Many months after the war we would come to realize just how heavy the losses were.

Of approximately 61,000 Dutch, English, Australians, and Americans forced to work on the railroad, 13,300 — 21 percent — perished. Of 270,000 Asians, 90,000 died. Next to the holocaust in Europe, the inhumanity displayed at Burma ranks with the worst in recorded history.

Those with Captain Fitzsimmons were lucky. Thanks to Dr. Hekking, only thirteen out of 194 were dead — less than seven percent. It was the best report of any of the doctors in the sixty-five slave labor camps along the railway.

More prisoners were to die before the war ended eighteen months later. But there would be no comparison to the number lost during the fourteen-month ordeal in Burma-Thailand from October 30, 1942 to January 12, 1944.

Jimmy Gee was with the group that eventually sailed for Japan. The filthy transport hugged the Indochina coast, sailing generally northward under the protection of coastal antiaircraft guns, then finally turning eastward for the treacherous run to Yokohama. The ships in the convoy loaded with prisoners carried the Japanese flag, not the flag or markings of the Red Cross. And some, including an aircraft carrier loaded with several hundred prisoners, were sunk by American bombers. The ship Gee was on made it through, thanks to a snowstorm that lasted just long enough to cover the ship's approach to Japan.

Gee and the group he was with were made to work in coal mines during the last eighteen months of the war.

I was with the group jammed sixty men per boxcar in Bangkok, Thailand, taken to the nearby docks, and shipped out by steamboat at night down the long, winding Mekong River to Saigon, French Indochina. We were imprisoned directly across the street from the Saigon docks and warehouses, both targets for American bombers. We worked on nothing but bomb targets — oil storage tanks, radio stations, an oil refinery south of Saigon, an ammunition storage warehouse in the heart of Saigon's industrial district, the airport two miles north, and further on north in a rubber plantation where we hid thousands of fifty-five-gallon drums of aviation fuel beneath the rubber trees.

For one stretch of time a group of us were put on a train and taken to Natrang, then up in the mountains to Dalat. We rode in a red caboose. The train was attacked by an American bomber, but apparently it had already dropped its bombs. All he did was strafe. And he missed. How that incident got mixed up with the other caboose scene in my nightmare is beyond me.

We were taken back to Saigon after we dug some bomb shelters for Japanese officers in the mountains near Dalat. Constructing blast walls of dirt, again using *yo-ho* poles as we had in the Burma jungles, accounted for much of the work we did. We built horseshoe-shaped walls at the airport where Japanese airplanes were parked. We built circular dirt walls around a dozen temporary radio broadcasting stations, and we dug holes twenty feet deep where radio equipment would be protected from bombs. We constructed the largest blast walls of all around huge gasoline storage tanks. Each wall we built was sodded with grass so spy planes couldn't spot it. Our work was of little value to the Japanese, as it turned out: we lived to see with our own eyes the kind of damage American dive bombers could inflict on such installations, regardless of blast walls.

The greatest danger we faced in Saigon was not from the Japanese as much as it was from our own Air Force, which day after day, month after month pounded the city from high level. Our B-17s and B-29s encountered heavy barrages of antiaircraft fire, to be sure. But the bombings were inaccurate, missing obvious targets by five or six entire city blocks with thousands and thousands of bombs. Not one ship was sunk in the harbor, until one day a lone Air Force B-25 came in low enough to drop a bomb down the hold of a freighter in Saigon River. The huge oil refinery was never hit by the Air Force. Nor were the high-octane gasoline storage tanks; nor the acres of fifty-five-gallon drums of gasoline hidden in the rubber plantation. (Later, near the end of the war, all of these were destroyed in a single day by dive bombers from U.S. Navy carriers, who by then must have had reliable intelligence reports.)

Bert Page, Lieutenant Lattimore, and Doc Hekking were among the group kept in Thailand as a part of the railroad maintenance contingent. And there was a further splitting up of prisoners: Doc was no longer with any of the Americans. He was sent to a camp in Thailand to administer to an Australian unit. He liked Australians, but he missed his American friends, particularly Bob Hanley and Slug Wright, his medical aides. To make matters worse, somewhere in the many moves they had made, he had lost his most prized possession: the painting of May on the piece of canvas. He had kept it rolled up inside a section of bamboo, which he had carried for hundreds of miles across sea and jungle, through some of the most godforsaken conditions known to man. And now it was gone.

One morning in early September, without explanation, Doc and the Australians were taken by truck to Kanburi, Thailand, to a prison camp on the edge of an airport. Doc did not know until he got there that twenty-one of his American friends were already there.

As he got off the truck, two Americans came running, waving a section of bamboo. He recognized Avon "Blue" Scarbrough and William "Shorty" Ingram.

"We got your wife! We got your wife!" they were yelling.

They pulled the piece of canvas out of the bamboo section and started waving it in the sun — the painting of May!

Doc gathered them into his arms, tears filled in his eyes.

At Kanburi, without warning, the Japanese announced that World War II was over.

It was as blunt as that.

The prisoners wanted to believe it. But there was nothing to prove it had actually happened. The guards still had their rifles. They were still around, watching.

One day, though, the prisoners noticed that some of the guards were missing. Then someone spotted a group of guards stealing away into the night. For the first time, the prisoners began to feel the joy of being free. But they weren't going anywhere; in a sense they were still captives. It was too early to celebrate.

To their credit, a few guards stayed, determined to return the prisoners to their respective nations in an orderly manner, no matter what the consequences.

The war might be over, but for Doc pain and misery were still around, and his job was to help wherever he could. Bert Page was suffering, his legs covered with angry tropical ulcers. These were not like the one on Glen Self's leg, or the one Jesse Bumpass had had on his foot.

"I'd like to try something different," he told Bert, inspecting the sores. "Do you mind?"

"Go ahead. Nothing can hurt any more than I hurt already."

It was mid-afternoon when Doc drew blood from Bert's buttock into a syringe — then injected the same blood into his legs where the ulcers were.

The pain was terrible. "Good Lord, Doc! Why'd you do that?" he cried.

"Don't worry. This is a treatment they used in France many years ago. It won't kill you."

Bert wasn't sure. By dark, he was in agony. He could not move his legs. It was the worst pain he had ever endured, without the benefit of being able to pass out.

Several hours later, the pain began to ease. Hours after that, he decided he might live. Two days later, the sores were beginning to heal.

Excitement reached a peak as an Allied warplane painted white came over and dropped leaflets telling them the war was over and the Americans would soon be coming in. "Don't eat anything unless you see it cooked, do not antagonize the Japanese" were among the instructions.

Doc read the leaflet.

"Fantastic!" he said. But all he could think of now was finding his family, even as he kept on working.

An Australian scalded his legs when boiling water spilled from a cauldron. Doc had nothing to use, not even leaves for a poultice. He told the man to urinate on the burns.

"Pee on me own legs? Gaw blimey, guvner!"

"Go ahead. It will be *soothing*," Doc said.

Sure enough, it was. And there was no infection, no scars.

Dutch prisoners were moved into camp along with British and Australians. The commander of the Dutch group came to talk to Doc.

The war was not over for the Dutch, he said. The Dutch had a problem in Indonesia: President Sukarno and his communist cohorts had taken advantage of World War II to start the long-expected revolution. "We need every man we can get," Doc was told. "You will conclude your affairs here and prepare to leave with us."

Lady Mountbatten arrived in camp, driven in a Jeep by British. When the Americans told her that if it had not been for Doc Hekking they wouldn't be alive, she asked to see him.

An American tells the story: "Poor Doc," he said. "No one told him she was coming. There was the wife of the Supreme Allied Commander of Southeast Asia, shaking his hand, thanking him for the splendid job he had done, smiling in her royal benevolent fashion, and there was Doc looking down, suddenly realizing all he had on was a pair of skivy shorts. But then, considering the shape the prisoners were in, so skinny and all, it's doubtful she even noticed."

Then one glorious day the Americans arrived.

Giant four-engine transports lumbered down from the clear sky, touched the ground, and one by one grumbled along the narrow runway toward the tower and the crowd of bony prisoners. They bore the white stars and bars of the United States Air Force.

Henri sensed they would not refuel. There would be no departure ceremony; they would spend only as much time on the ground as it took to get his friends aboard. He went immediately to one of the planes to say goodbye, thinking it might be many years before he would see his boys again.

They were young, they had exciting new lives ahead of them. They were lining up around the steps leading to the open door. He knew the joy they had to be feeling. But he couldn't shake a feeling of sadness that increased by the minute. He had learned to respect and love these boys — no, they were men now. Soon, in a matter of minutes, they would be out of his life, and already he had the hollow feeling of loss. A lump formed in his throat as he shook their hands.

"Goodbye, Slug. Thanks for your sunny disposition. Take care of yourself," he said.

Slug started to shake hands. He threw his arms around Doc instead. "You'll find May and the kids, I know you will. I'm gonna miss you, Doc. If there's ever any way I can hep you —"

"Thanks, Slug."

"Come on with us, Doc!" Fitzsimmons said, wringing his hands. "We'll fix it with them bureaucrats so's you can stay. Come on — we'll set you up in your own practice! We'll be your first patients!"

"Yeah," Lattimore said. "We're not pulling your leg. Remember, you're talking to a bunch of Texans!"

"That's what I'm afraid of."

"Most of us will be in Texas. We kid you not," Bert Page said. "They's enough of us to keep you going."

"Me, doctor you crazy Texans? Never!" Tears glistened in Hekking's eyes.

"Come on, Doc! Don't just stand there!" someone called from the doorway.

"You crazy guys! What are you trying to do, get me hanged for deserting my army? You know I can't leave without my family. You know I have to find them."

Lattimore waited until the others were aboard. "We'll never forget what you did," he said. "Without you, we wouldn't be here."

One by one the planes moved down the runway into the wind, gathering sky beneath their wings, reaching toward the heavens, pulling themselves up, their engines a great symphony.

Lattimore later related to me the atmosphere within his departing plane. The men looked at one another, out the windows, and at one another again as if in disbelief.

It was not a dream, it was actually happening — they were free, they were going home!

An American crew member was walking the aisle handing out luncheon boxes: the first bread, butter, and milk they had seen in forty-three months. They held on to the boxes, too overwrought to eat.

Free! Free — and going home!

Emotions were turning inside out.

Looking down, Lattimore saw the solitary figure beside the runway, waving. Like one of his own men left behind, the last man out: a man they would return for, sooner or later, he was certain.

He swallowed hard. He waved back, knowing the man couldn't see him. Tears welled in his eyes and the image was blurred.

"So long, Doc," he muttered. "Thank you. God bless . . ."

18

The Search

Several months elapsed before anyone knew what had happened to Doc Hekking.

Repatriated Americans had a country to return to, unscathed by war, and we were eager to get on with our lives. There was no medal for having been a prisoner, but we were treated as returning heroes. Once we were out of hospitals and back in uniforms, displaying the rows of combat and service medals — the Presidential Unit Citation for those of the USS *Houston* — we could not walk on the streets in our hometowns without our emaciated bodies telling the story (most of us had lost over one-third of our original weight); without people offering to buy drinks and meals. We were paid at the rate of our last held rank for the forty-three months in prison camps, then bumped up one notch in rank. We were given a choice of staying in the service with still higher rank, or of taking honorable discharges. Individually, we were written up in newspapers and interviewed on radio. It was as though the people of the United States could not do enough.

We reacted in different ways. Drugs were not a problem in those days, although alcohol was, and it frequently was used as a sedative to quiet the tidal waves of emotion. None of us expected the sudden adulation, and some were unable to handle it. Some were on psychological roller coasters, riding to monumental highs then crashing — unable to cope with families, friends, jobs, education, new careers, or life itself.

Dr. Hekking had no country to return to immediately after the war.

Holland was occupied by Hitler's troops, and its government was in exile in England. Even after the government was once again fully in the hands of the Dutch, much of Holland was in ruin. To finance reconstruction, the government borrowed heavily from the United States through the Marshall Plan. So did other Allied European countries. Holland was determined to be the first to pay back its debt, and succeeded in doing so.

But the Dutch government's handling of the men who had served it well left something to be desired. As late as 1987, there was still controversy about the way it had awarded back pay to its servicemen who had spent time in prisoner-of-war camps. For example: when the war ended, all soldiers of the KL, The Netherlands' regular army, received full back pay. This applied even to those few who were stationed in Indonesia. Royal Dutch Navy personnel were similarly paid regardless of where they were stationed. However, soldiers of the KNIL, the Royal Netherlands Indies Army, were awarded substantially less pay since most of the enlisted personnel were natives of the islands. When they complained, they were told by the government that they should get the remainder of their pay from the new dictator, Sukarno.

Doc was kept in KNIL, his assignment to continue serving as an army doctor — never mind the fact he still had not found his wife and children. The revolution was in progress on the islands, a bloody affair at times. And he was right in the thick of it, treating wounded, while we were back in the States trying to adjust to a life of so-called serenity.

Doc missed his friends, as well as his family. He took time to write to one of our group in Texas, saying it was the only address he had of any American, and he would most certainly be pleased to know how the crazy Americans were getting on. He was still trying to find his family. But he wondered: were we sticking to the diet he had suggested? Would this fine Texas boy pass the "old jungle quack's" address around and suggest to some of the boys that he missed them and would like to hear from them?

The soldier thought it was a nice thing for Doc to have done, writing like that. He set the letter aside, fully intending to answer it. It was thirty-five years later before he got around to it — and he suggested in his letter that he would appreciate an answer as quickly as possible! Doc laughed about it, and he wrote to the man immediately, kidding him about the long-lost mail. Of course, the revolution had long since ended by then, and Doc was back in The Netherlands.

Slug Wright knew nothing about Doc's letter to Texas. He had used his back pay as collateral to start an auto service station in Oceanside, California, saving some to launch a search for Doc. He was well on his way to establishing himself in business at the time Hekking wrote that first letter (and the last one to anyone for some time), and he was already beginning to contact various ex-prisoners of war, trying to find out if anyone knew how to reach Dr. Hekking and/or his wife and children.

Unfortunately, the one man Slug did not contact was the man in Texas.

Otto Schwarz took a job with the post office in Union, New Jersey, and he too began to reach out — first to locate other ex-POWs, then to try to find Dr. Hekking. A wire service reporter heard about Otto's search, and he wrote a story that appeared in various languages throughout Europe: "Americans Search For Their Wartime Hero." Although Otto had no way of knowing it at the time, the story was read by Queen Wilhelmina of The Netherlands.

Slug contacted the embassy of The Netherlands, setting forth his own version of the facts about Doc's success in saving the Americans' lives. Further, in his best Texan language, he reckoned as how the Queen of The Netherlands would surely want to honor one of her country's own doctors who had put his life on the line for fourteen months to save the lives of his fellow Dutchmen, as well as Britishers, Australians, and Americans on the Burma-Thailand Railroad. He put it in writing to the Dutch Embassy.

The "ranch in Texas" was not to be for Gee, Page, and me.

Gee enrolled at The University of Texas in Austin and married the daughter of a United States diplomat to South America. He thought often of the other ex-POWs and of Doc Hekking, and he was determined to help organize annual get-togethers of the survivors and, sooner or later, to find Doc and bring him to the United States.

I went back to Kansas with the thought of finding my stepfather and dealing with him once and for all — possibly giving him a dose of his own blacksnake whip.

I sent a telegram to my mother, telling her when I would be arriving at the railroad station in Hutchinson and suggesting that she meet me.

When I got off the train, Jim was there instead, waiting in the old red 1936 truck I had hauled wheat in when I barely knew how to drive. Jim got slowly out of the truck as the train was pulling away, and I stood there in dress blues, holding the overseas bag, watching him, feeling the crowd surge around me.

Jim waved and yelled. "Hey, boy, is that you? Over here!"

I went toward him, a hollow feeling in my gut. There was none of the anger I thought I would have. No bitterness. Nothing.

He held out a hand. "Welcome back."

I shook hands. The hand was no longer rough. "Where's Mom?"

"At th' farm. Wanted me to pick you up. Thought maybe you and me would — well, talk. You know?"

I tossed the overseas bag up behind the cab. "Talk about what?"

We got in and started down through the main part of Hutchinson. There was not much traffic. The street and buildings looked the same.

"The old town has changed. See how it's changed, boy?"

I looked out at First National Bank. And across the street at Wiley's. At Fox Theater. At Gus Meschke's.

"I've changed too, boy."

I studied his face out of the corners of my eyes.

"Yep, I've changed." A stream of tobacco juice went out through the window, a part of it staying on his chin. "Gettin' older. Ain't well no more. Diabetes, I got. Heart trouble, too, I got. And my stomach. Bad stomach."

"Sorry to hear it."

We drove on in silence for a while, on through South Hutchinson, onto the diagonal road southwest toward Partridge.

"How was it, boy?"

"How was what?"

"The war, dammit! You kill some of them Japs? Hey? You kill some of them slant-eyed sonsabitches?"

Several moments elapsed. "There's a field between here and Partridge," I said. "You know the one. That's where I want you to stop this thing."

He turned pale. "Why would you wanna stop?"

"When you threw me out, you thought you'd killed me, didn't you?"

"No, boy! I didn't think that! Nosiree!"

"Stop the truck," I demanded. "Right here. This'll do. Pull over."

He did as he was told, bringing the truck to a tired halt.

"Them days is gone, boy! I ain't like that no more! What you gonna do? You ain't gonna —"

I sat staring at the cruel face, the face I hated. "I've waited a long time," I said.

"What you gonna do, boy?"

I just sat there, letting the memories flood back. Then suddenly the man beside me was older looking, bloated, sick — pathetic.

"Drive on," I said.

He let forth an audible sigh and used a red bandana to wipe the back of his neck. "You wanna come work with me, boy? You and Mike, you'll inherit th' place some day, you know."

"Go to hell," I said.

I regretted being so harsh with Jim Evans. After all, he was abused by his own father, so what could Mike and I have expected from him? Fortunately, I made my peace with him long before he died in 1964.

But at that time, right out of prison camp, I was still filled with hate for Jim Evans. I didn't know it then, but I was on the verge of collapse. I ended up in Great Lakes Navy Hospital.

The Americans didn't know where our prison camps were in Saigon. They were unmarked, adjacent to prime bomb targets, the warehouses of the docks. Bomb shelters for prisoners in Saigon were nothing more than rice paddies, inadequate even if one could reach them before the bombs fell. Our prison compound was sur-

rounded by a twenty-foot-high fence made of four-inch diameter
lengths of bamboo poles tied solidly together all the way up. On
platforms mounted on each corner were guards with machine guns,
and pillboxes were placed around the outside of the camp with machine guns pointing in toward us, knee-high. There was one gate
that opened out on the rice paddy. I couldn't get to it during one
particular air raid. I had reinjured my knee and couldn't walk. So
after I fell in the attempt to get through the gate, they shoved me
back inside. Thousands of pounds of bombs pounded along the
river, missing their targets, thundering along the street, destroying
a tobacco factory, burying people alive . . .

The diagnosis they gave me at Great Lakes Naval Hospital
was "combat fatigue," caused by too much stress over too long a
period of time. But I felt like a phony who had seen very little combat. I couldn't consider the prisoner-of-war experience in the same
breath with combat, because we weren't shooting at anybody. Of
course, we were down there underneath our own American bombers day after day in Saigon for eighteen months; we existed on the
thin edge between life and death for forty-three months. But that
wasn't combat.

President Harry Truman had his hands full bringing the GIs
home from overseas. They were arriving in droves, many heading
for hospitals, some with symptoms like mine.

I remembered the little amenities people in civilized circles
took for granted, but I was not comfortable, using a knife and fork,
trying to remember that pants were to be zipped, that toilets were
to be flushed, that car doors and doors to buildings were to be
opened for females, that money was to be kept in a checking account which one had to know how to balance. I was awkward with
all of those things, and it bothered me. My body was loaded with
hookworms and I could not gain weight. I was fleeing from something, I knew not what, although there was no longer anything to
fear or run from. I was nervous because I was nervous. It was like
an echo chamber, my voice cloned a million times. The nightmare
about the caboose became a nightly affair.

"Time will help. In fact, it is the only medicine," the navy doctor said. "Try to put the war behind you. You are still young.
You're a survivor, you've proved that. Don't look back. Don't talk
about it. Try not to even think about it. There are nicer things to
think about."

Easily said. Not so easily done.

The armed services were not equipped to deal with returned ex-prisoners of war, beyond feeding them high-potency vitamin pills, a well-balanced diet, and providing them with the opportunity to rest.

The returned ex-prisoners, like others leaving the armed services, were busy building careers, trying to make up for lost time, shoving grade averages sky-high on college campuses across the country. The economy was booming: it was an unprecedented era when anyone could make it if he could walk upright and think reasonably straight. Jim Gee, a marine friend of ours named Hugh Faulk, and I were trying to adjust to college life — Jim at The University of Texas, studying for a teaching certificate; Hugh at Oklahoma University, preparing to be a petroleum engineer. I was in Northwestern's Medill School of Journalism.

We knew Doc Hekking was somewhere in the thick of Sukarno's revolution. Where, we were not sure. We were stretched to the breakpoint.

One of Slug Wright's friends went to San Francisco and returned with a copy of a Dutch newspaper translated into English. In it was a story which mentioned Hekking's name. Through that lead, as slender as it was, Slug managed to get a letter through to Indonesia with the right address. And Henri at last knew that the Americans had not forgotten him. He wrote back to Slug immediately. And Slug shared the correspondence with Otto Schwarz and Jim Gee, and they in turn passed the word along: "He's alive!"

As we read copies of Henri's letter, the mosaic came together: a tangled picture of deaths, heartaches, and disappointments for the Dutch; of exuberance turning to disappointment and hatred of the Japanese for the Indonesians.

Many younger Javanese men in the East Indies had gone berzerk after World War II ended. Men who were gentle and quiet before the war were torturing and mutilating, carrying out atrocities to equal and exceed those perpetrated by the Japanese. Called *"peloppors"* by the Dutch, they were armed with Japanese weapons, had learned the art of killing from the Japanese, and had added bizarre methods of their own.

The British urged the Dutch women to take their children and flee to the safety of prison compounds, because the weak and unprotected were the *peloppors'* primary targets. One woman was racing for a prison gate, carrying her baby, and a young madman caught up with her just before she reached it. He snatched the baby from her arms. The gate slammed shut behind her, and seconds later the bloody head of her baby came hurtling over the fence, onto the ground in front of her.

British General Louis Mountbatten, Supreme Allied Commander in Southeast Asia, was receiving the surrender of Japanese armies in all of the Nippon-occupied territories in the area, including Indonesia. This British control created misunderstandings among the Dutch, who were hurriedly putting together their own army to quell Sukarno's forces. Mountbatten may have been sympathetic to the Dutch problem in Indonesia, but England's real enemies — Germany, Italy, and Japan — were vanquished, and there was no enthusiasm for further conflict.

In fact, the British offered little help to the Dutch women and children on the islands until the *peloppors* killed a British general. This enraged the British, and they promptly dispatched Gurkhas and Sikhs to take on the *peloppors*. Unfortunately, in some instances this was like throwing gasoline on the fire because the sympathies of some of the Gurkhas and Sikhs were with the Indonesians. To this day, there is still bitterness on the part of some Dutch soldiers who claim the British would not allow them to defend their women and children: stories still persist that the Gurkhas turned their backs while *peloppors* took women from the camps, raped them, and killed them.

Throughout the East Indies, without help, the Dutch controlled the major communications and shipping facilities of military importance. Not once were they ever in serious danger of losing the islands militarily, despite the fact that if one believed what he read in newspapers and magazines or heard on radio, Sukarno's forces were winning. The problem was, sentiment in most capitals of the world was against the Dutch, and somehow in favor of what was perceived to be a small band of Indonesians fighting for the most noble cause of all — freedom. At least most Javanese thought they were fighting for freedom. But Sukarno at best was a dictator, and there was no freedom.

The United States was against the spread of communism, but

it was also against colonialism. Its attitude was like that of Great Britain: the real enemies of freedom were already vanquished.

So, without help, the Dutch continued to contain Sukarno. Because they maintained control of transportation, they kept industry going virtually uninterrupted, even while Sukarno was making it look to the outside world as though the islands were in chaos. Sukarno could take comfort in what he perceived to be the world in his corner. No one was coming to the aid of the Dutch. So why shouldn't he fight on? He won, ultimately, not by defeating the Dutch on battlefields, but by forcing Holland through world opinion to hand him the islands on a silver platter.

There were many Dutch and Indonesian casualties in sporadic attacks by revolutionaries. The Dutch Colonial Army was brought in, and Henri and the other Dutch ex-prisoners of war were kept in uniform without back pay and with no rest or recreation. Some of them were so weak they could barely hold their rifles.

Henri was assigned wherever he was needed most urgently, with no official time off to try to find his family. In desperation, and without permission, he ultimately conducted his own search through Indonesia, now ravaged by the revolution.

It was quite a different story for his American friends who had gone home to an atmosphere of peace.

I had my own automobile at Northwestern University. I lived in a furnished three-room apartment on Farwell Avenue just south of Howard Street, thanks to the GI Bill and forty-three months of back pay. Among my chief concerns were learning how to conduct myself sanely in civilized circles again, coping with cold weather and clothing and sore feet (it took more than twelve months for the thick calluses caused from going barefooted to come off the bottoms of my feet), and above all, trying to learn how to study again.

Already, the revolution in Indonesia seemed unreal and far away, and somehow unrelated to Doc Hekking.

But it was real to Doc. The Japanese had taken thousands of able-bodied Indonesians to Thailand to work on the Thai-Burma railroad and on other war-related projects. And when Japan surrendered, there was an immediate tangle of population movements — hundreds of Indonesians going to the new railroad in search of missing family members, hundreds more coming back in the opposite direction, back to the islands, trying to pick up where they had left off. Doc talked to many fresh from Indonesia, trying to find someone with knowledge of families held captive on Timor.

It was a frustrating, futile time, one lead after the other becoming a dead end. There were the terrible rumors, one persisting that the Japanese had killed their prisoners. He would hear that, and agonize with despair; then there would be a rumor that rekindled hope.

He learned that May's father, Dr. van Hengel, had died during the German occupation. The Germans had taken over the van Hengel house and had carted away most of the family's precious antiques. May's mother, Marie, was still alive. The house itself had not been damaged. She had gone back there to live.

An elderly Indonesian was certain Henri's mother had died in a Japanese prison camp in Tjimahi, Java. He also said he was sure Henri's brother had died in Burma; that May and the children were safe and in Makassar, Celebes, living near the Dutch Colonial Army Hospital.

Henri had been disappointed so many times he hesitated to believe this man. He was about to walk away.

He turned and walked back. "What did the lady look like? Tell me again," he asked.

"She was very thin, with dark brown eyes and dark hair."

"How tall?"

The man held his hand at eye level — May's height. Somehow Doc knew it was the truth.

The man's descriptions of Fred and Loukie were amazingly accurate. Doc's heart began to pound.

How did they come to Makassar? Did the old man know that?

He wasn't sure. He had heard that the leader of a wild tribe — Towana, he believed it was — had come down from the hills to deliver the women and children to safety. The Towana's leader had a name with the sound of the Middle East — Abdul, he believed it was. A bold man; a daring, determined man.

At the risk of being killed by revolutionaries — or of being punished by the Dutch army — Henri bluffed his way aboard a Dutch ship bound for Makassar. It was under the command of the British, who were still in control of Indonesia. It didn't matter who was in control to him, as long as he got to Makassar.

And the old Indonesian was right.

He found May, Fred, and Loukie — five months from the day

he had started the search. They were with four other women and eight children living in a house near the Dutch Army Hospital.

May was sick and so weak she could barely walk. She was terribly thin. She staggered as she got to her feet, tears streaming down her cheeks. He tried not to let her know how shocked he was as he stood for an instant, looking. The children too were thin and undernourished, but they appeared to be well.

He took May in his arms and they held each other, saying nothing, weeping with joy.

19

Message From Texas

Doc was not well, yet he didn't complain as he went from one duty assignment to the other. With each move, the army helped him settle into decent quarters with his family, which he fully appreciated. But now they were sending him on missions connected with the revolution, and his life was in constant danger.

One assignment was to Salajar, an island south of Celebes, a high-risk area. Fortunately, his time there was brief. He was senior medical officer of the army hospital at Balikpappan, East Borneo. May was hospitalized there. Her recovery was slow — too slow. He was anxious to get her back to The Netherlands for special treatment, but she was too sick to make the long voyage home. He managed to send Fred back aboard a Dutch evacuation ship, and arranged to have him stay with his brother (Fred's uncle) so he could resume schooling. He would not be able to send May and Loukie back until 1947, nor could he return himself until a year after that.

He knew what was wrong with his back: the blows administered by the Japanese had broken and cracked several vertebrae which were not healing properly. But he had never complained, as long as he could move about. A medical discharge now, while he was still a captain, would mean that he would retire with a pension level based on that rank, which was not enough to live on and take care of his family.

It was in the Makassar Hospital in 1946 when he first suspected his American friends were up to something. He and six other doctors were called into the main office, where the chief medical officer of the region stood with a piece of parchment in his hand. The doctors were told to stand in two rows, four in back, three in front. Doc stood in back. The paper the officer held in his hand looked like a certificate.

"I've called you here because I have a message from the Queen," he said. He allowed the significance of his announcement to sink in, then added: "One of you will receive a medal."

The doctors looked at one another, wondering who had been singled out. "It's for you, I'm sure," Doc said to the man standing next to him.

The chief medical officer looked directly at Doc. "I don't know why you got it, but here it is," he said, presenting the parchment. "Go ahead, take it. It's yours."

It was the certificate of the William of Orange Award.

Doc was as astounded as the others, who were now shaking his hand.

The ceremony was finished. There was no medal — he would receive that later on. It would include a gold emblem of crossed ceremonial swords, if he were willing to pay for it.

"I am advised of contributions you made to members of the armed services of The United States," the colonel was saying. Doc smiled inwardly, his mind racing back to the slave labor camps, to the image of a grinning Slug Wright. Slug was behind this, he thought to himself. He was right.

Rather than buy the crossed ceremonial swords, Doc informed the Dutch government that he would prefer that the money be used as his contribution toward the purchase of a used Jeep, which he could drive around to various small villages on Celebes to administer medical services where they were badly needed. He ended up without a Jeep, without the crossed swords.

Doc arrived in The Netherlands without fanfare a year after

May did and went directly to the Amsterdam Institute of Tropical Medicine. May had gone to one of Holland's leading internists for diagnosis and was being treated for liver problems.

Hekking was eventually promoted to major, even though the black mark still on his record forestalled further promotion. He knew that, regardless of how he felt, he had to stay in active service for one year as a major before he could retire with a pension at that rank. So he suffered it out, with injuries and poor health directly attributed to the slave labor camps in Burma. Eventually, he was able to retire.

He was never critical of the Royal Dutch Colonial Army. If it had ever occurred to him that the army had treated him unfairly, he never said so. He spoke only in superlatives: "The best intelligence-gathering service in the world . . . ," "the toughest discipline, necessary for the toughest fighting men in the world . . ." he would proudly state.

"Maybe others might think I was wronged. I don't think so. I was young, so very young . . ."

Henri and May lived for a time in a four-story house that May's grandfather had owned. He had his medical discharge, but he was not retired. In 1950 he accepted a job as medical appeals officer with the Dutch Ministry of Defense, a post he held until 1971, when he retired. He would be sixty-eight that year, and he and May would settle into a small apartment in The Hague, not far from Leiden University. In his retirement he would give lectures before medical classes at the university; have access to books and current medical papers; and meet as often as he chose with those who could keep him abreast of the state of the art in medicine.

But he was feeling a void in his life, having severed the close relationships that had grown in prisoner-of-war camps. He missed his friends more than ever. He was not close enough to attend their reunions.

Several years went by and, aside from Slug Wright's regular letters, it was not often enough that he heard from the others.

Doc was depressed. He blamed part of it on growing old.

And then one beautiful day in spring a letter arrived from the United States, postmarked Dallas, Texas, April 11, 1956. The return address was to J. W. Gee.

Eagerly, he opened the envelope. The letter read in part:

Dear Dr. Hekking —

There is never a time when two or more ex-P.O.W.s get together from our group (from the U.S.S. *Houston* and the 131st Field Artillery) that you are not mentioned . . .

. . . The combination of your kindness, skill and energy was the torch . . . You helped us to realize that happiness was not in our circumstances but in ourselves.

. . . I have been asked to write to you to see if you would accept an invitation to be our guest at our next convention to be held in Mineral Wells, Texas, in early August, this year. We will furnish round trip tickets . . . we will take care of hotel accommodations . . .

Sincerely,
James W. Gee

"What is it?" May asked.

Henri smiled, his eyes brimming. "Do you realize we have never seen the United States? Perhaps now it is time . . ."

20

Dallas: August 9, 1983

"Are you sure this is what you want?" Marti asked before we called the travel agency.

"Yes. Doc Hekking will be there."

What she was referring to was the upcoming 39th Annual Reunion of the "Lost Battalion" in Dallas.

The camaraderie that had grown among survivors of the USS *Houston* and men of the 131st Field Artillery extended into civilian life, encompassing families, close friends, and offspring. It was truly unique. They started what they called the Lost Battalion, and held their first reunion in 1945. The reunion still is held every year, always in Texas, always in early August, as close as possible to the date we were liberated.

I had gone to only one before, the one held in Mineral Wells in August 1956 — that first year Jim Gee called to say they were bringing Doc over from The Hague.

One could have fried bacon on the sidewalks of Mineral Wells that summer. I arrived in the heat from Chicago and spent a few minutes talking to Doc and his son Fred. I sat up all night in the hotel lobby talking to Gee and Page and left with a terrible hangover the following morning. And the problems with nerves returned.

I was not back to normal again for a year, and I promised myself I would never go to another reunion. For twenty-four years I kept that promise, immersed in business, determined that the war would not be the biggest thing that had ever happened to me. Work became an obsession. I became successful beyond anything I had ever dreamed possible for a kid who had come from the Ozark Mountains barefooted to Kansas, and had run away from home at age sixteen.

And then came the word from Jimmy Gee that Doc Hekking would be at the August 1983 convention, possibly for the last time. Doc, after all, was eighty.

In 1978, the year the nightmares returned, Marti and I sold controlling interest in the company we owned. She would continue working in something else, but for health reasons I had had to retire. So we were able to come and go more or less as we pleased, and we flew to Dallas.

We arrived at the Crown Plaza Hotel an hour before noon. I tossed my luggage in our room and went directly to the lobby. For a time I avoided the tables where men were registering in. I wanted to test the water, to see how I felt about being there before I fully committed myself to staying.

I was supposed to know these men. Yet the only way I could identify them was to walk embarrassingly close, throw my head back, and look through the lower parts of my glasses, peering like a fool at name tags with too-small lettering. The men I stared at didn't recognize me. They probably thought I was just an incredibly rude guest of the hotel, not connected with the reunion.

But Packrat McCone knew who I was — even without eyeglasses.

He yelled halfway across the lobby. "Hey, Charlie!" Hundreds were eyeing me now, and it made no difference. There we were, two old codgers wringing each other's hand, worrying about the other's arthritis, muttering things that made no sense.

"Charlie?" someone behind me asked.

The voice was unmistakable. I swung around. "My lord — Bird Dog!"

We were hugging each other, laughing. "My God, what a sight for sore eyes!"

I had to register in after that; to put on the name tag for others to squint at. And to ask the expected: "What did you do when you got out?"

Bird Dog was in the petroleum business: the guy taking oil off super-tankers from the Middle East once they anchored off New Orleans. It was a nerve-wracking business, directing oil to different storage areas, hoping one didn't goof.

What ever happened to John Wisecup, the guy who almost made it with the Boston Red Sox? He got the ultimate revenge on the Japanese: he married one!

"But what about you, Charlie?"

It was not a comfortable feeling, trying to explain why I had stayed away so long. "Sick," I said most often. And to those who pressed me, I added: "The war affected some more than it did others." And I dropped it at that. Who could argue?

I had caught up with just about all of them, and I felt more at ease when the noontime banquet started. I had only to contend with those at the large round table where Marti and I and our family sat. Both of our daughters had married Texans, and they were there with their husbands and children — our granddaughters. And there was the one strange man who came to join us without introducing himself.

Jimmy Gee and his wife Shirley were at the far left end of the speakers' table. Retiring soon as vice president-sales of one of the world's largest paper products companies, Jim was in charge of the Dallas reunion. He still had his dark flashing eyes, his dark wavy hair. POW life obviously had not affected him physically.

Marine Corps Capt. Charles Pryor was coming in to take his place with the speakers. He had stayed in the Corps, and was in the Korean conflict as well as in Vietnam. He was minus a leg, yet busy helping others at the Veterans Administration hospital in Dallas, not moaning about his own loss. And he was an assistant professor at one of the universities in Dallas.

Adm. Arthur Maher with his wife Betty were taking seats to the right of the speakers' table. Maher was the gunnery commander who came down from the top of the main mast to order Standish and me to abandon ship minutes before the *Houston* sank.

Otto Schwarz and his wife Gertrude were arriving at the head table, and Otto was rapping the gavel. Nothing about him was reminiscent of the "Dead End Kids." He was a retired executive with the post office, and editor of the ex-prisoners' newsletter since the end of World War II. He still had the same New Jersey accent, the same quick sense of humor.

Senator John Tower, chairman of the Armed Services Committee, was also at the head table. I knew what Tower had promised to do when he got back to Washington, D.C.: He would stand before the Senate to read the report about Doc Hekking — a report that would live forever in the *United States Congressional Record.*

That was Slug Wright and his wife Lou, talking to Otto and Tower. Slug was a successful businessman; the former mayor of Oceanside, California. Near him stood Henri Hekking's son Fred. Tall and dark like his father, Fred had the same heavy eyebrows and dark eyes. He was an engineer with one of the nation's largest aircraft manufacturers, and was an American citizen, thanks to the help of Slug and Lou.

I was distracted by the man sitting next to me, shoving a newspaper under my nose, pointing to a story on the front page. It was the kind of thing the media did each August, reviewing the awful effects of the two atomic bombs dropped on Japan by Americans. And now there was something else: The United States was being asked to compensate Japanese-American citizens for the way they were treated in the United States during the war.

"What about the treatment of prisoners of war by the Japanese?" the man next to me wanted to know. "Didn't people know about those slave labor camps? Everyone knew about the way the Germans treated prisoners in Europe during World War II. But didn't they also know about the way the Japanese treated their prisoners?

"Every August, people of the United States were supposed to take their annual guilt trip because they had dropped those atomic bombs, killing a hundred thousand Japanese. But didn't anyone know about the hundred thousand people the Japanese starved to death, tortured, and killed along the Burma-Thai railroad? Why not publicize that annually too?

"Were we trying to forget the enormity of the Japanese atrocity? If so, then why weren't we trying to forget the holocaust in Europe? If there was any logic in keeping alive the memory of gas chambers and atomic bombs, then why wouldn't the same logic apply to keeping alive the memory of what happened on the Burma-Thai railroad?"

We listened to the man's questions. They would haunt us for the rest of our lives, I suppose. We had no answers.

We were grateful when the rumbling noise began, of people moving chairs, getting to their feet. The applause started as Doc and May came in a side door and started toward the head table. He was eighty years old, but he looked younger as they walked along the edge of the room, smiling, waving. He was attractively thin, tanned, healthy, and happy looking. She was radiant and dignified in a conservative dark dress. His hair and heavy eyebrows, once black and bushy, were snow white. The lines of his face were a little deeper than I remembered. But his movements were sure, and his voice as vibrant as ever as he spoke to a full room of his "boys" and their families.

"I am a lucky fellow," he said, eyes twinkling. "All my life, I am lucky fellow. I was born in Surabaya, Java, to very fine Dutch parents who came there from Netherlands. I can go to very fine medical school in Netherlands. I can do that when most of my Javanese friends cannot, so I go to Leiden University, not too far from Amsterdam. I am lucky to meet this beautiful lady, May, who becomes my wife. We have two beautiful children. Then comes the war and all is hopeless.

"May and my children are taken away from me by the Japanese on Timor. We lose our country, The Netherlands, to Nazi invaders. We lose our beautiful East Indies, our lovely islands, to the Japanese. The Japanese take me into Burma jungles to slave labor camps where you and other prisoners are building the railroad. Men are starving and dying of sickness and I have no instruments and no medicine. I have nothing. I am very depressed. I do not wish to live because I see no future. Then one day, a crazy American came into my life, and you all came.

"You are prisoner like I am, you are hungry like I am — yet you are laughing and singing, and if you are not happy then I know you must be crazy. Very crazy. Pretty soon you have me laughing with you, and not thinking about myself but about you, and of course I begin to think I am crazy too. You teach me to speak and cuss in what you say is English and what I find out later on is Texan, not English — not even very good Texan. People in Europe

who speak English, they do not understand what it is I am saying
anymore. Which sometimes is perhaps a pretty good thing.

"You do me a great honor telling me I saved your lives, when
it is you who saved my life, for which I am very grateful, you see?
You tell me I had something to do with inventing psychosomatic
medicine. It is nice thing for you to tell me that, but I tell you that
what you think was psychosomatic medicine was hocus-pocus I
learn from my *oma*, my grandmother, when I lived with her for a
few years when I was a little boy. She treated sick natives in Java,
and sometimes she would talk to them this hocus-pocus, and sometimes it made them well — if they believed it, which many of them
did.

"Well, later on when you and I were together in Burma, it
wasn't so much what I learned in Leiden or in Bergamo or Batavia
that could help. It was what I had learned from my grandmother,
my *oma* — that was what I could do something about. There was
only the jungle, no pharmacy, no medicine, nothing. We have each
other, we have this thing we share. And we have the jungle and
things which *Oma* knew . . ."

Doc's words had a soothing effect. I realized then how much I
had missed the men, and I knew that from then on I would come to
the reunions as often as I could. And I knew it was also possible
now for the first time to start writing the book.

Looking toward the line of windows, I imagined the sun coming out as it had so many years ago on a warm, desperate afternoon. Doc was weaving his spell again: the room was changing, the
men and their wives were young, and the world was bright and
promising.

Appendix

A. Speech delivered by Lt. Col. Y. Nagatomo to Allied Prisoners of War at Thanbyuzayat, Burma on October 28th 1942

It is a great pleasure to me to see you at this place as I am appointed Chief of the war prisoners camp obedient to the Imperial Command issued by His Majesty the Emperor. The great East Asiatic war has broken out due to the rising of the East Asiatic Nations whose hearts were burnt with the desire to live and preserve their nations on account of the intrusion of the British and Americans for the past many years.

There is therefore no other reason for Japan to drive out the Anti-Asiatic powers of the arrogant and insolent British and Americans from East Asia in co-operation with our neighbors of China and other East Asiatic Nations and establish the Great East Asia Co-Prosperity Sphere for the benefit of all human beings and establish lasting great peace in the world. During the past few centuries, Nippon has made great sacrifices and extreme endeavors to become the leader of the East Asiatic Nations, who were mercilessly and pitifully treated by the outside forces of the British and Americans, and the Nippon Army, without disgracing anybody, has been doing her best until now for fostering Nippon's real power.

You are only a few remaining skeletons after the invasion of East Asia for the past few centuries, and are pitiful victims. It is not your fault, but until your governments do not wake up from their dreams and discontinue their resistance, all of you will not be released. However, I shall not treat you badly for the sake of humanity as you have no fighting power left at all.

His Majesty the Emperor has been deeply anxious about all prisoners of war, and has ordered us to enable the opening of War Prisoner camps at almost all the places in the SW countries.

The Imperial Thoughts are unestimable and the Imperial Favors are infinite, and as such, you should weep with gratitude at the greatness of them. I shall correct or mend the misleading and improper Anti-Japanese ideas. I shall meet with you hereafter and at the beginning I shall require of you the four following points:

(1) I heard that you complain about the insufficiency of various items. Although there may be lack of materials it is difficult to meet your requirements. Just turn your eyes to the present conditions of the world. It is entirely different from the pre war times. In all lands and countries materials are con-

siderably short and it is not easy to obtain even a small piece of cigarette and the present position is such that it is not possible even for needy women and children to get sufficient food. Needless to say, therefore at such inconvenient places even our respectable Imperial Army is also not able to get mosquito nets, foodstuffs, medicines and cigarettes. As conditions are such, how can you expect me to treat you better than the Imperial Army? I do not prosecute according to my own wishes and it is not due to the expense but due to the shortage of materials at such difficult places. In spite of our wishes to meet their requirements, I cannot do so with money. I shall supply you, however, if I can do so with my best efforts and I hope you will rely upon me and render your wishes before me. We will build the railroad if we have to build it over the white man's body. It gives me great pleasure to have a fast moving defeated nation in my power. You are merely rubble but I will not feel bad because it is your rulers. If you want anything you will have to come through me for same and there will be many of you who will not see your homes again. Work cheerfully at my command.

(2) I shall strictly manage all of your going out, coming back, meeting with friends, communications. Possessions of money shall be limited, living manners, deportment, salutation, and attitude shall be strictly according to the rules of the Nippon Army, because it is only possible to manage you all, who are merely rabble, by the order of military regulations. By this time I shall issue separate pamphlets of house rules of War prisoners and you are required to act strictly in accordance with these rules and you shall not infringe on them by any means.

(3) My biggest requirement from you is escape. The rules of escape shall naturally be severe. This rule may be quite useless and only binding to some of the war prisoners, but it is most important for all of you in the management of the camp. You should therefore be contented accordingly. If there is a man here who has at least 1% of a chance of escape, we shall make him face the extreme penalty. If there is one foolish man who is trying to escape, he shall see big jungles toward the East which are impossible for communication. Towards the West he shall see boundless ocean and above all, in the main points of the North, South, our Nippon Armies are guarding. You will easily understand the difficulty of complete escape. A few such cases of ill-omened matters which happened in Singapore (Execution of over a thousand Chinese civilians) shall prove the above and you should not repeat such foolish things although it is a lost chance after great embarrassment.

(4) Hereafter, I shall require all of you to work as nobody is permitted to do nothing and eat at the present. In addition, the Imperial Japanese have great work to promote at the places newly occupied by them, and this is an essential and important matter. At the time of such shortness of materials your lives are preserved by the military, and all of you must award them with your labor. By the hand of the Nippon Army Railway Construction Corps to connect Thailand and Burma, the work has started to the great interest of the world. There are deep jungles where no man ever came to clear them by cutting the trees. There are also countless difficulties and suffering, but you shall have the honor to join in this great work which was never done before, and you shall also do your best effort. I shall investigate and check carefully about

your coming back, attendance so that all of you except those who are unable to work shall be taken out for labor. At the same time I shall expect all of you to work earnestly and confidently henceforth you shall be guided by this motto.

Y. Nagatomo
Lieutenant Colonel, Nippon
Exp. Force

Chief No. 3 Branch
Thailand POW Administration

B.   Presidential Unit Citation to USS *Houston*

THE SECRETARY OF THE NAVY
WASHINGTON

The President of the United States takes pleasure in awarding the PRESI-
DENTIAL UNIT CITATION to the
UNITED STATES SHIP *HOUSTON*

for service as set forth in the following
CITATION:

"For outstanding performance against enemy Japanese forces in the
Southwest Pacific from December 7, 1941 to February 28, 1942. At sea almost
constantly, often damaged but self-maintaining, the *Houston* kept the sea. She
maneuvered superbly and with deadly anti-aircraft fire repulsed the nine-
plane Japanese Bombing squadrons attacking a troop convoy under her escort. Later, in company with other Allied ships, she engaged a powerful
enemy force, carried the brunt of the action with her two remaining 8 inch
turrets and aided in damaging and routing two enemy heavy cruisers from the
line of battle. On February 28, the *Houston* went down, gallantly fighting to
the last against overwhelming odds. She leaves behind her an inspiring record
of valiant and distinguished service."

For the President,

s/Frank Knox

Secretary of the Navy

C. Americans Interned with Dr. Hekking

Last Name, Rank, First Name, Middle Initial
*Died since World War II, some with health problems related to PW camps
**Died in PW Camp

Agin, F2c Gerald L.
Anderson, Pvt. Luther L.
Anthony, Pfc Nolan D.
Argabright, Pvt. Joseph H.
Armstrong, Pvt. Roy G.
Arnold, S2c Floyd
Arroyo, Pvt. S. G.*
Ashworth, Pvt. Hix*
Aust, Jr., Pvt. Richard
Bailey, Pvt. Jack W.
Bain, S1c M. L.
Ballew, S2c James
Barnes, Pvt. Daniel F.
Barnes, S2c Stanley D.*
Beardsley, S2c Marvin M.
Beatty, S2c Paul E.
Bedford, S1c W. J.
Bender, S2c George F.**
    5/22/44 dysentery
Bergen, S2c James T.
Betancud, Pvt. Santos L.*
Bigger, S2c Delwone B.*
Black, S2c Arthur R.*
Blackwelder, Pfc Alton J.*
Bowers, Pfc Walter A.
Bowley, R. J.
Brain, S2c Donald*
Branum, Pvt. Dalton*
Brimhall, Pfc Clifford
Brimhall, Pfc Onis L.*
Brinker, Pvt. Harold

Brothers, S1c F. W.**
    11/8/43 malaria
Bukowsky, Pvt. Emil G.
Bumpass, Pvt. Jesse F.
Butler, Pvt. Jesse W.*
Campbell, Corp. Charles J.
Carpenter, Pvt. Lonnie J.
Castro, S1c M.
Chapman, Pvt. Henry E.
Chapman, Pfc William J.*
Charles, Pfc Howard R.
Childers, S1c M. K.*
Clark, Pvt. John D.
Clark, Pvt. Braxton*
Clay, Pvt. Joseph F.
Clay, Pvt. Melvin L.
Clendenen, Pvt. J.
Cole III, Pfc J. B.
Combs, Pfc Dale V.
Cooper, Pvt. James M.*
Crain, Pfc Drew W.
Cray, Pfc Hampton R.
Curley, Pvt. Laverne
Dalezio, Pvt. Frank**
    12/23/43 beriberi
DeMoss, S2c Donald D.
Derrick, Pvt. Cecil L.
Dethloff, F2c Robert L.
Dickens, Pvt. William H.**
    1/1/44 beriberi

Dickenson, Pvt. Wilburn**
   cause, no information
Dove, Pvt. Miley
Drake, Pfc Leonard H.
Eastham, Sgt. Ramon G.
Eichorst, Pvt. William C.
Eklund, Pvt. Rudolph L.**
   1/28/44 dysentery
Elam, S2c Richard W.
Elliott, Pfc E. L.
England, Pvt. Clifford J.
Ewing, S2c James C.*
Falk, Pvt. George A.
Fay, S1c M. L.*
Fenrick, Pvt. Harlin F.*
Ferguson, F2c John A.
Fitzgerald, F2c James
Fitzsimmons, Capt. Arch*
Forrester, S1c J. E.
Forsman, S1c M. L.
Frasier, Pfc Harold R.
Frie, Pvt. Marion L.
Frie, Pvt. James W.
Fung, Pfc Edward
Galbraith, Pfc Stanley
Galowski, F2c Leon H.
Garcia, Pvt. Alfred C.*
Garcia, Pvt. Jose J.
Gee, Pfc James W.
George, S2c Perlie M.*
Gillen, Pfc Earl H.
Glazner, Pfc Thomas H.
Gnat, Pvt. Frank J.
Gregg, Pfc Roy L.*
Gregg, Pvt. Robert N.
Grice, Pfc Walter L.
Griffith, Pvt. Hubert
Gunnerson, F1c C. F.
Guzzy, Pvt. Walter
Hallandy, Pfc Mathew J.*
Hammack, Pfc Zack
Hammons, Pvt. Roy H.*
Hanley, S2c Robert L.
Hanser, Pvt. Charles*

Harris, Pvt. Dewitt
Hensley, Pvt. Jim E.*
Hicks, Jr., Pfc J. M.
Higginbotham, Pvt. H.
Hiner, Lt. David A.
Hird, Pfc Hilton E.*
Hofstutler, Pfc Other*
Holten, Pfc Melvin*
Hoover, Pfc J. W.
Huebler, Bug. E. A.*
Huggins, Pvt. George
Ingram, Jr., S2c William
Jordan, Pvt. Roy E.
Jordan, Pfc Willie V.
Kenney, Pvt. Robert W.
Kershner, Pvt. Horace V.
King, Pfc Ray W.
King, Pvt. F. H.*
Ladwig, Pvt. Lawrence
Laird, Pvt. John M.
Lamb, Pfc Floyd R.
Landin, Pvt. Mariano
Lattimore, Lt. James
Lawley, Pvt. George F.
Leatherwood, Pvt. Ellison
Ledbetter, Pvt. Jimmie*
Lewis, Pfc Dale A.
Long, Pfc Luther J.
Maher, Pvt. Boyd E.*
Martinez, Sgt. Homero
Matlock, Pvt. Sidney
Mattfeldt, Pvt. William F.**
   11/16/43 heart
May, Pfc Richard*
McCone, Pfc James
McElreath, Pfc Jessie*
McFarland, Pvt. Thomas
Medina, Pfc. Refugio
Morris, Pfc James R.*
Musto, S2c James W.**
   7/17/43
Netter, S1c Jack G.
O'Brien, Pvt. John F.*
Ogle, Pvt. Ray

Oliver, Pvt. Garth S.
Oosting, Pvt. Charles*
Owen, Pfc John H.
Owens, Pfc Floyd I.
Page, Pfc Bert E.
Paquin, S2c James*
Pfeil, Pvt. Stanley A.**
    cause, unknown
Pitts, Pvt. Jennings B.
Pitts, Pfc Caston**
    1/14/44 beriberi
Polidoro, S2c Vincent
Quick, Pvt. Fred B.*
Ray, Pvt. James E.
Ray, Jr., Pvt. George F.
Rayburn, Pvt. Eldridge L.
Rea, Pvt. Maston L.
Reichle, Pfc Grover
Roberts, F2c Valdon S.
Robinson, Pfc Marvin E.
Rogers, Pvt. John W.**
    1/28/44 dysentery
Ross, Pvt. George E.
Ross, Jr., F2c William*
Schwarz, S2c Otto C.
Scroggins, Pvt. Herman W.*
Self, Pvt. Glen B.
Sherill, Pfc Cosby H.

Shuster, Pfc John F.
Simpson, Pvt. Ward**
    tuberculosis
Smith, Pvt. J. W.
Smith, S2c James
Smoke, Pvt. Albert F.
Solomon, Pfc Henry W.
Spencer, Pvt. Thomas J.
Stambaugh, Pvt. Clyde M.
Stensland, Lt. Roy*
Stone, Pfc Preston E.
Teal, Pvt. Horace G.
Teborek, ? ?
Tidwell, Jr., Pvt. Walter M.
Torp, Pvt. Franklin
Trice, Pfc Ernest M.
Vinge, F2c Harold M.
Wade, Pvt. Arnold W.
Wampler, F1c C. A.*
Warcken, S2c Augustin
Wehring, Pvt. Theodore
Willey, Pvt. Lloyd V.
Williams, Pvt. Carl H.
Wilson, Pvt. James R.**
    11/17/43 malaria
Wolf, S2c Joseph W.
Wood, Pfc Chester L.*
Wright, Pvt. Houston T.

Bibliography

Barnouw, A. J. *The Making of Modern Holland*. New York: W. W. Norton & Co., 1944.

Costello, John. *The Pacific War — 1941–1945*. New York: Rawson, Wade Publishers, Inc., 1981.

Fischer, Louis. *The Story of Indonesia*. New York: Harper & Brothers, 1959.

Forster, Harold. *Flowering Lotus — A View of Java*. London: Longmans, Green & Co. Ltd., 1958.

Mintz, Jeanne S. *Indonesia — A Profile*. Princeton, NJ: D. Van Nostrand Co., Inc., 1961.

Pinder, David. *The Netherlands*. Boulder, CO: Westview Press, 1976.

United States Congressional Record. Vol. 129, No. 161, November 18, 1983.

USS *Houston* Survivors Association. Archives. Union City, NJ.

Vlekke, Bernard H. M. *The Story of the Dutch East Indies*. Cambridge, MA: Harvard University Press, 1945.

Wigmore, Lionel. *The Japanese Thrust, Australia in the War, 1939–1945*. Sydney, Australia: Halstead Press, 1957.

World Book Encyclopedia. Field Enterprises, Inc.

Interviews, Correspondence

Dr. Henri Hekking; his wife, May; son, Fred; daughter, Loukie; son-in-law, G. F. Olaf Belinfante — with the author at The Hague, Netherlands.

Prisoner of War Group 2, including survivors of USS *Houston* and of 131st Field Artillery interned in camps with Capt. Arch L. Fitzsimmons and Dr. Henri Hekking.

Dr. Henri Hekking (with sword and plumed hat) with May Van Hengel, and wedding party just prior to their wedding. Henri was commissioned first lieutenant in the Dutch Colonial Army in October 1929, and he and May were married a few days later.

— Photo courtesy Dr. Hekking

The voyage on a luxury liner from Europe to the Dutch East Indies in November 1929 was to serve as a grand honeymoon for Henri and his new bride, May. They were on their way to Batavia (now Jakarta), Java.

— Photo courtesy Dr. Hekking

Batavia Military Hospital, Batavia, Java, as it looked when Dr. Hekking arrived for his first assignment in the Dutch East Indies.

— Photo courtesy Dr. Hekking

The radja of Kolonodale, Celebes (man in the center), shown with his entourage, thought Henri was "crazy" to search in the mountains for Towana natives who were ill, when it was the Towana who killed white people with blowguns. Henri had gone to Kolonodale for "punishment duty," but he made his stay there a fulfilling, learning experience.

— Photo courtesy Dr. Hekking

Dr. Hekking made the rounds administering to sick in a wide area around Kolonodale, Celebes, and he was soon to become the natives beloved "papa." He was often given receptions by leading officials of various provinces. A radja, center, and two of his aides form this welcoming party in the village of Boengkoe August 1931.

— Photo courtesy Dr. Hekking

Kolonodale Military Hospital as it was in 1931 when Henri was there on "punishment duty." Located on the east coast of Celebes Island, Kolonodale was occupied by only ten Europeans (or half-castes), a few Chinese, and about 400 friendly, intelligent natives, mostly of Toradja stock.

— Photo courtesy Dr. Hekking

May made only two trips with Dr. Hekking during their four-year stay on Celebes. Here, helped by Lapakiri and a recalcitrant horse, she crosses a jungle stream near Kolonodale to make the rounds.

— Photo taken by Dr. Hekking in 1932

The Ruth *drops anchor off Kolonodale, bringing supplies from Java, letters from The Netherlands, and hospitality extended by the ship's captain. Inter-island ships like* The Ruth *were also used twice a year to help Dr. Hekking make medical services available to ten small islands off the coast of Celebes, also within the area of his responsibility.*

— Photo courtesy Dr. Hekking

Lt. Adrie Nouwen, left, was a regular military officer and the only other Dutch Colonial Army officer at the Kolonodale post. He and his family pose with the Hekkings in front of the Hekking house near Kolonodale, June 9, 1932. May is sitting between Nouwen and Henri, holding daughter Loukie.

— Photo courtesy Dr. Hekking

Dr. Henri Hekking, May, and their children, Fred, left, and Loukie, in front of their Kolonodale house. Life in Kolonodale was miserable for most officers assigned here prior to Henri's arrival, but Henri made the Celebes a learning experience in tropical medicine — an experience which later helped save the lives of hundreds of prisoners of war.

— Photo courtesy Dr. Hekking

A patrol sets out from base hospital, Kolonodale garrison, in 1932. Their mission was to provide health care to natives in surrounding villages.

— Photo courtesy Dr. Hekking

Madoekala, center, Dr. Hekking's orderly, with the head of the local village of Boeng-koe, Celebes. Henri always offered as much training to an orderly as the orderly was willing to accept, thereby extending health care on the islands.

— Photo courtesy Dr. Hekking

Dr. Hekking poses with some of his patients at Malang Hospital, Malang, Java, in 1931. Henri's parents lived in Malang and died there during World War II.
— Photo courtesy Dr. Hekking

The first view one would have coming in by ship to the village of Kolonodale, Celebes, in 1930. There was only one house made of brick in the village, and a regular army officer and his family lived in that — not the Hekkings. The first thing one saw at the dock was a graveyard.
— Photo courtesy Dr. Hekking

Dr. Hekking and his family in front of the house assigned to them at Kolonodale. As a part of his effort to make the best of the situation, Henri had a swimming pool built near the house.

— Photo courtesy Dr. Hekking

In April 1939, Henri and May sailed from Surabaya, Java, to Italy via Netherlands aboard a luxury Dutch ship which boasted a swimming pool. He rated a twelve-month furlough to The Netherlands. But instead of going there, he opted to study surgery for one year with a famous Italian doctor at Milan University, Bergamo, Italy.

— Photo courtesy Dr. Hekking

Henri and May entertain in their small apartment (small by American standards) in The Hague. They and their children were not reunited until five months after World War II ended. She was seriously ill when he found her, and the children were dangerously undernourished.

— Photo courtesy Dr. Hekking

Dr. Hekking with two of his grandchildren, Loukie's children, in Voorschokten, Netherlands, January 25, 1970.

— Photo courtesy Dr. Hekking

Dr. Hekking in his office at The Hauge Hospital, in 1962. Hekking was eventually promoted to major in the Dutch Colonial Army, despite the black mark on his record. But in order to qualify for a major's pension he had to be on active duty for two years with that rank. So he stayed on in service after World War II.

— Photo courtesy Dr. Hekking

Although Dr. Hekking retired at seventy with dignity and honor from the Dutch Colonial Army — this photo was taken on the day of his retirement — the black mark was never expunged. But the Queen of The Netherlands was to learn of his contributions to prisoners of war, thanks to his American friends from Texas.

— Photo courtesy Dr. Hekking

"I am a very lucky man. I have always been a very lucky fellow," Dr. Hekking said repeatedly, even when things were at their worst. His feelings of optimism and his love for his fellow man had a way of permeating people around him, bringing them sooner or later to his own more cheerful, hopeful point of view.

— Photo courtesy Dr. Hekking

Henri and May took a sentimental voyage in 1963 aboard the same kind of ship that in 1929 had taken them on their honeymoon voyage to the East Indies. He was an exceptional ballroom dancer — so good, in fact, that once, in his teens, he declined an opportunity to become a professional dancer. When they visited Dallas, Texas, in 1983, they danced together at the annual Lost Battalion reunion.

— Photo courtesy Dr. Hekking

Henri with two of his son Fred's children, Fred Jr., and Janet, in 1963. Fred became an American citizen and is employed with an aircraft manufacturer working on NASA's space platform projects.

— Photo courtesy Dr. Hekking

The author, H. Robert Charles, with Dr. Hekking, right, in Delft, Netherlands (September 1985).

— Photo by author

The Japanese did not mark prisoner-of-war camps in Saigon, French Indochina, and they forced the prisoners to work on airports, oil refineries, oil storage tanks, docks, ammunition storage depots, and radio stations around the city. There were no reliable intelligence reports coming out of the area, thus the American pilots of B-17s, B-25s, and B-29s had no idea that they were bombing their own people when they raided the city.

— Photo courtesy Otto Schwarz

Photo of half the marine detachment of the U.S.S. Houston *taken aboard ship in Manila Bay a few weeks before World War II started. Half of the men shown here survived sinking of the ship and prisoner-of-war camps. J. W. Gee is on the back row, fifth man from the left, and directly in front of Gee is the author, H. Robert Charles.*

— Photo courtesy of the author

A few of the Marine survivors of the U.S.S. Houston *with Dr. Hekking in Mineral Wells, Texas, in 1956. Back row, left to right: James W. "Caribou" Gee, Frank H. "Pinky" King, Dr. Henri Hekking, H. Robert Charles, Charles Pryor, and James "Packrat" McCone. Front row, left to right: Marvin Robinson, Bert "Bird Dog" Page, Lloyd Willey, and Walter "Shanghai" Grice.*

— Photo courtesy of the author

INDEX